"*Nobody Else Has Complained,*" Or Are You Just Not Listening? 25 Ways To Be Better In Business

Chris Heitzman

"Nobody Else Has Complained," Or Are You Just Not Listening? 25 Ways To Be Better In Business

Chris Heitzman

Academica Press
Washington~London

Library of Congress Cataloging-in-Publication Data
Names: Heitzman, Chris (author)
Title: "Nobody else has complained," or are you just not listening? : 25 ways to be better in business | Chris Heitzman
Description: Washington : Academica Press, 2024. | Includes references.
Identifiers: LCCN 2024936202 | ISBN 9781680533279 (hardcover) | 9781680533286 (e-book)

Contents

Chris Heitzman is a senior lawyer and has been a Partner in two national UK law firms. What does a lawyer know about entrepreneurship? Chris is certainly not just another lawyer in the sense of being the man in the corner who tops and tails the precedent paperwork when the entrepreneurs in the room have done the real work. He was made Partner at the age of just 34. He has founded and led teams, had front-line responsibility for sales, and managed major client relationships. He was assessed by an international firm as having 'no business development needs' in his early thirties. Soon after another firm said he was better at sales than its sales director. He has seen business from the perspective of running law firms, and from advising and working closely with a range of businesses from small entrepreneur-led start-ups to boards of major public companies. He is also the author of the polemic 2021 Academica Press release, *The Coming Woke Catastrophe*, which examined woke culture and sought to guide the West through the turbulent waters of the irrational ideology. Chris is a proven thought-leader, and now applies his entrepreneurial vision and knack for speaking out to give new insight and help to anyone interested in business in 2024 and beyond. The examples in the book are loosely taken from stories the author has heard, from the business news pages, and some are fictional. They are dramatised for the sake of storytelling and illustration.

Foreword

There are many business books that address the big issues in business. They will tell you that cash is king. They will tell you about converting leads, and maximising margins. If you have the vaguest interest in business, you will probably have read it all before. Not that those fundamentals are not important: of course they are. My interest in being involved in and advising businesses has been beyond the basics: the transition from a zombie business, trading, perhaps solvently, but making money or surviving by luck rather than judgment, to becoming a great business. The things that make the difference between just plodding along on the one hand and really acing it on the other.

So this is not just another business textbook, that regurgitates all the basics, either in a stale or new way. It instead focuses on some specific ways to be better in business that you may not have thought of. It aims to give fresh food for thought. Is your business just a zombie business? Or is it performing to the best of its true potential?

Business might still survive, and make money, by ignoring all of the advice herein. But my ethos has always been that just good enough isn't good enough. If you are going to participate in business, you may as well fulfil your full potential, rather than just survive. The two often involve similar time and effort. The difference is doing it right.

Why now? With the cost of living soaring global conflicts and other challenges, and some economies performing averagely, people are cutting back, or being more discerning about how and where they spend their money. There is still demand in most sectors, but the businesses feeling the pinch the most are those who, frankly, were coasting in a fog of mediocrity in better times. You can get away with mediocrity in boom times. But in tighter times people will be more choosy and more careful about where they put down their dollars.

Your business might be underperforming – and may begin to struggle in pinch times – because it is making mistakes and failing to seize opportunities which, until now, have gone unseen. This book collates some of the less well written about lessons the author has learned in business. Individually or collectively, they could boost your business – or your contribution to the business you work for – from average to great, and that difference can be the difference between success and failure, especially in times when money is squeezed by living costs.

Indeed, all of this is more relevant now than ever before. We live in a world where there are more businesses, delivering more competition and more choice. Every year more businesses start-up. Every year the best businesses get better. To thrive, and increasingly to even survive, in a competitive and mature business world, just 'good enough' is not good enough, and instead an ethos of constant improvement is necessary.

I want everyone to thrive as we emerge from lockdowns and battle the new challenges, and if this book even in some small way can contribute to business surviving in tough times then it will have done its job.

The chapters are short as they each focus on an individual idea. You can tackle them in any order you like. You can skip some, and dwell on others. Whatever works for you.

1

Introduction: Nobody else has complained

You're wondering about the title of this book so let's get to that one first.

A team leader once alerted a national operations director in a company to the fact that an entire team had been without IT for the first 3 hours or so of the working day.

So, to the operations director's reaction. It was, as the title of this book suggests, *"Nobody Else has complained."* The instinctive reaction was not to want to jump on identifying the cause or the solution to the problem, but to instead simply observe that this was the first complaint about it.

And if the reaction missed the point, it was also factually misguided too, because it wasn't the first complaint. For many hours around 100 people or more across the business had been complaining. The ops director's first knowledge of the problem was when someone decided it was time to make a complaint to senior management. The best the operations director could in truth say is that nobody had complained *to that person.* To have been ignorant of the wider noise did not mean that people were not complaining, but merely that the ops director was not listening.

The culture was to muddle along, be slow to spend money on a solution, to use existing resource when that had already proven lacking, and to hope it might resolve itself. Meanwhile, the best competitors were parachuting in the best people and kit to deliver a platform that was as close to 100% stable and reliable as possible, to ensure its people could work whenever they needed to. Despite the effort and spend associated with that, their customer retention and profits were higher because the spend and effort paid for itself many times over in outcomes.

But to suggest an investment is to take a risk. To be seen as someone proposing to add cost, as opposed to bringing in revenue. But that is the blooper of complacency: good business often starts in identifying a return on potential investment, or in solving a problem. If doing nothing and hoping for the best seems easier, it is probably so only in the short term. Doing nothing, failing to invest, not doing it properly, is likely a much greater risk than rising to a challenge and doing it properly.

And the executive who says where is the problem I haven't heard too many complaints only appears incapable. Perhaps he has his earplugs in, or has mastered selective deafness to preserve his own energy. The competent leader is always listening, and solves challenges before the complaints flood in.

Perhaps counter-intuitively complacency can be most dangerous when things are good. It might have taken an absence of complacency to get into a good place, to start things off, to secure business relationships, to make a return. But when things are good the risk is that complacency sets in either because of a perception that things are good so we can ease off now, we've earned the right to take it easy, or because further risk might be dangerous to the success achieved. How many people on fat salaries have you met with a business idea to go it alone, but who never do it because the temptation of the fat salary is too big for them to take a risk, go it alone, and potentially achieve many times the success and freedom and control they ever would as an employee. Some success makes people complacent. Even if the opportunity cost is something better. A good situation makes people happy enough to settle. But the risk is that a good enough situation prevents greatness. Beware complacency, in good times and bad.

It got me thinking. What mistakes do businesses frequently make, without even knowing it. Could businesses be bumping along thinking, 'we're doing ok because nobody has complained.' Some businesses could be doing ok, with nobody positively complaining, the business generating enough cash to pay the bills, but they could nevertheless be badly underperforming. It was the inspiration for this book. Together in the chapters that follow we will explore other topics that might be holding you back in business that you may not have thought of.

It is human nature to over-estimate our own abilities. It is a survival trait. If you surveyed a hundred businesses on how well they think their business was going, I bet very few if any would jump to tell you what they are doing badly. They would, naturally, want to tell you what is going well and about the business' achievements. Almost every business will tell you it is the best in its sector. The only thing that makes people think things could be better is when something goes obviously wrong. People reappraise a business when it starts losing money. Or when complaints start flooding in. And often even in those scenarios businesses are slow to react, and incomplete in their response. After all, if they knew the solutions they probably wouldn't have got it wrong in the first place.

I instinctively dislike the pursuit of just 'good enough.' I always ask instead, how can it be better? I would credit any success I have enjoyed to that trait above others. To slip into a mentality of 'that'll do' or 'everything is ok' is, in business, and possibly other areas of life too, to allow things to flat-line, to be good but not great, and, in a competitive world, to allow competitors to catch up and get ahead. The best businesses are not lazily waiting for complaint or crisis before they examine their performance. They are instead proactively listening to their businesses using a doctor's stethoscope, and every day asking how can things be better, and ever-improving. They aren't waiting for a complaint to identify a way to improve: they are looking for it anyway.

So, what are people in your business not complaining about, that could be very much better? If you shake off any lapse into 'that'll do' or 'it's good enough,' reach for the stethoscope, and really listen to your business and ask what can be better? These are the invisible advantages of asking what could be better, even in the good times, rather than bumping along complacently waiting for complaint or disaster to wake us up. You can think of it as listening, but for the almost imperceptible noises, rather than waiting for the loud noise of complaint or disaster. In the example of the IT failure given above, it might have been prevented by the ops manager asking, long before the failure, 'is our IT world class? Is the hardware modern, robust and as fast as it can be?' The ops manager might have done some proactive listening, by asking IT specialists, and tapping into the practical experience of people around the firm. Rather than waiting for complaints as the first sign there might be a problem.

TIP

Ask yourself how good every aspect of your business or role is. And then after answering critically analyse your own answer with fresh eyes and ears. Challenge yourself. Even if nobody is complaining, or if superficially things look ok, is that alone or good news story? Or if you look and listen – *really look and listen* – can you find ways to be better? And if you find ways to be better, how might implementing those improvements raise your game and benefit your outcomes? Avoid numb complacency and instead develop a sensitivity to ways in which you can boost any aspect of your business, and see the difference this change of approach can make to performance. Don't be so complacent as to think waiting for complaints is the time to look and listen: do it before the complaints start and you might avoid them.

****

2

Be an astronomer rather than a mathematician

Formula One motor racing history bores will recall Alain Prost's nickname 'the professor;' so called because of his famously numerical approach to racing. In his own words, *my ideal is to get to pole with the minimum effort, and to win the race at the slowest speed possible.* His great rival, the late Ayrton Senna, however, knew only flat-out racing. Prost would slow down if the second-placed man was 30 seconds behind. Senna would instead try to build that lead from 30 seconds to 60! Prost would see a 60 second lead as a waste of energy; Senna would only be satisfied with his maximum performance, regardless of what everyone else might be doing. To Prost a win by 1 second was good enough; to Senna only his maximum potential being fulfilled was good enough. To put labels on things, perhaps Prost was the mathematician and Senna the stargazer.

What can we learn from this in the world of business? I have seen plenty of examples of goods and services being obviously bred from a culture of striving only ever to be just 'good enough.' Nothing spectacular. But good enough to nevertheless sell. I've seen some cars, for example, with inconsistent panel gaps, a poor paint finish, bits of trim loose, and a driving experience as miserable as having a tooth filled. However, such cars sell, in high volume, and generate a handsome profit for their owners.

Producing something relatively rubbish instead of something spectacular involves a significant saving of time and money. One needs fewer (if any) quality controllers, less time is spent on design and engineering, and so on. Maybe, in profit terms, the 'good enough' model can make more profit for its owners! Good enough products can get to market quicker than perfected ones, and will be cheaper to produce thus limiting the cost side of the balance sheet. The 'good enough' model is also less taxing on its owners: they don't wake up in the middle of the night worrying about how to be even better. If a lot of customers don't notice some of the ways in which better products are better, such improvements may be entirely wasted.

However, the 'good enough' model is always at greater risk. The threat from competition is much hotter. Take Senna's 60 second lead, for example: from such an advantageous lead, he could have a blown tyre and a failed front wing, pit twice and still win the race. Prost's mere 1 second lead, if it suffered such bad luck, would put him down out of the points scorers. Equally, the mediocre motor car might sell until a rival makes one slightly better, then it might stop selling completely. The danger from being only just ahead is that a small lead can be eroded very quickly.

The image and reputational risk is also greater for the 'good enough' business, and the sales pitch isn't as easy. 'Good enough' isn't much of an advertising strap line is it. Certainly not such as easy sell as 'great.' Customer experience and word of mouth is likely to disproportionately hit average businesses in a negative way, whereas for the great business the opposite is true.

It may be a question of longevity. In the short term, 'good enough' might be a win for business owners. They might achieve sales and maximise profits by not performing better than is absolutely necessary. In the long term, 'good enough' in a competitive market is always likely to be overtaken by something 'better.' That is not to say short term thinking is always an entirely bad thing. Some of the richest people out there have got rich on obviously short-term business strategy, and perhaps not with the best product or service. Seizing a moment and enjoying it while it lasts. But generally striving to be the best you can be will endure beyond a business that stops at just 'good enough.'

TIP

Is a one goal advantage at half time enough? Is being five car lengths ahead in a grand prix at half distance enough? It may sometimes be. And in such instances with hindsight a 3 goal advantage or a 30 second lead might just look like 'wasted' energy. One goal or a five car length lead might have been 'good enough.' But the trouble with only ever being 'good enough' is you are likely a hostage to fortune. What if the other team makes a key substitution and score 2 goals in the second half? What if a different tyre at the next pit stop gives the second placed car a 1 second a lap advantage? Suddenly what was 'good enough' becomes not good enough, and instead of energy saved your problem is potential unfulfilled. If you aim to be your best rather than just good enough, you're more likely to get and stay ahead, in the short and long term.

****

3

Unconventional is good

Rarely is a business success story a conventional one. If for example you were planning to launch a new supermarket, would emulating an existing mid-market boring player be a great idea? You might launch such a business and wonder why aren't we doing great: we have copied another business doing ok. But are customers likely to be enlivened by another supermarket that just looks and behaves the same as the one they are already a little bored with? Probably not. It is an easy trap to fall into to think that 'playing it safe,' or keeping it conventional, is the route to success. Playing safe can seem less risky. But the failure rate among those who play safe will be high. The most successful businesses have been radically unconventional.

If you look at the success stories in business, they tend to be a bit 'out there' rather than boringly conventional. Look at the iPhone for example. It appeared when all other phones still had tiny black and white screens and a twelve button keypad with numbers and symbols on them. The iPhone by the market standard when it first appeared was whacky and unusual: a colour touch screen, no buttons save a home button, apps and the web. The rest of the market was making small improvements to age old technology. Apple for ahead by designing something entirely new from the ground up.

By way of further example, the first vacuum cleaner to catch dust without a bag soon sold – despite heated challenge from rivals – 8 units for each 1 sold by the rest of the market put together. Dyson couldn't sell its customers dust bags for its cleaners, like the rest of the industry could, but the success of its unconventional design meant it didn't need to. The rest of the market was still eyeing bag sales for mediocre machines, while Dyson got ahead by doing it differently.

The same is true not just of product, but marketing and business management too. In marketing, Sony's 'colour like no other' campaign used a short and simple slogan, with rhyming first and last words, to convey to anyone that no other TV had a colour screen as brilliant as a Bravia. It didn't try to explain, in boring technical terms, why it was better. A wider colour range, perhaps. A brighter backlight, possibly. A quicker processor. Who cares? Rambling on about the boring technical detail would have made them part of the crowd, rather than standing out from it. Likewise Skittles' 'taste the rainbow' campaign, capturing in just a few words the joy of a rainbow of joyous colours and tastes in a handful of sweets. They didn't talk about pack size, the flavours included or anything as conventional as that. A bold metaphor may have been unconventional, and therein lied its appeal.

In business management, in my own sector – law – the process of sifting papers in a document-heavy matter once took days if not weeks. Conventional thinking was that earning £350 an hour for reviewing and listing documents was good business. Right up until slicker rival firms introduced software with artificial intelligence that could do the job in a third of the time. Yes, the number of hours per matter might reduce, but at the gain of getting more instructions than slower, more expensive rivals, increased morale among lawyers reviewing documents, and spare time to invest in client relationship management or business development at even greater gain.

So if I was going to launch that new supermarket, perhaps doing it with unique brands, unavailable elsewhere, and with new in-store services, like freshly baked sourdough bread daily, or a counter for same day brilliant takeaway cook at home good, might be a way to be unique and different enough to succeed in an already crowded and arguably stale market. Be the Dyson or Apply in a market to get ahead, rather than just a small stake of more-of-the-same.

TIP

Avoid the illusion that a successful business must be as ordinary or sensible as the competition. Merely duplicating the dreary and derivative, at least in relatively established markets, is instead likely to be a short cut to mere mediocrity at best, and failure at worst. A successful enterprise usually does things differently to stand out and appeal from the crowd.

****

4

'The how' is what leads
to successful outcomes

Businesses sometimes speak of targets. So for example a car dealership might speak of achieving 250 sales per month. A department store chain might speak of achieving profits of £25 million per store. In my own profession, dispute resolution in the legal sector, we might speak of resolving a given number of claims, or litigating a given number of claims, or producing a given amount of fees per claim.

The trap for the unwary is to think that targets or desired outcomes are the answer and that success means just imposing those targets or outcomes on a business, and possibly monitoring delivery to targets thereafter. If success in business was that easy, everyone would be successful. I can easily say I want to sell 1000 units of a particular product a day at £5,000 a unit, and think that is a business plan. It is of course instead merely an ambition, without a plan!

So the rookie car dealership owner, who thinks all that matters is his targets, will save money by recruiting someone cheap who isn't great in sales, and will say to that salesman, 'right, there's your target: get on with it.' The rookie car dealership owner will be disappointed when the sales don't come in as expected, even if the target was perfectly achievable in the market. He will become frustrated with his salesman: you had your target: why haven't you delivered…! The rookie salesman will become frustrated that he's being asked to do more than is within his capability. The target alone will not have produced the desired outcome, in the absence of knowing 'how' it was going to happen.

The department store chain might open ten stores, in the wrong locations, full of the wrong goods, without the right level of in-store service, and the wrong type of store managers with a £25 million annual margin per store target. We all know by now: that business is not going to deliver that target. Nothing like it. Not without a 'how;' not without a plan how to achieve the ambition. The business has made the mistake of thinking declaring the target is all there is to business, as opposed to appreciating that getting the business model right is how you get to the target. So, stores in the right location, selling the goods local people want, with the appropriate people in the store to connect to the customers, might deliver the target.

In my own profession, the trap is to judge and promote lawyers based on their measurable performance against targets. So the lawyer who opens the most files, or settles the most, or puts the most time on each matter on average, might be seen by a target dashboard as the best performer. But what if what really drives success in law is having people who are technically at the top of their game, know how to interact with and manage client relationships on a highly deep and sophisticated level, and how to build and coach brilliant teams. You could fill a law firm with very average people who can deliver well on a few targets. But it may not be the law firm many clients want to keep returning to. The out-of-his-depth lawyer could recommend to clients (under) settling a few claims this afternoon, litigate a few unmeritorious claims (worry about the fallout later) and spending too long doing everything to increase time per file. Performance this week might look great if the targets were settlements, litigation and time recorded. But would it really be a good performance? I am more interested in lawyers getting the clients the optimum result, so that clients are always delighted with outcomes, litigating when it's the right step but not when it isn't, and delivering optimum financials by billing a level of fees clients think are good value but not over-charging and without write-offs from mistakes or non-payments. In other words, the lawyers with the skills and judgment that are going to, more often than not, deliver the right sort of results. That, beyond month one, is the more sustainable and more successful business model.

The lesson is that the strategy and ingredients for success – the 'how' – must come before the targets, not the other way around. Else you risk a rush to mediocrity at best, or failure at worst. The mediocre manager or business owner will rush to simple, measurable targets. Because it makes that manager's job easy. Tick box. But the better manager or business owner will realise that success in business is about more than just simple targets and is instead about creating a great business. Targets are how you measure business success. They are not how you *create* business success.

Ask yourself what is your business model. If it is 'to make £50 million profit this year,' without more, you might be in trouble, and you are unlikely to succeed. If on the other hand the business model makes reference to what is great about your product or service, the gap and your place in the market, and your capability, you've got a good chance of achieving good profits... maybe £50 million if that is achievable with the right model in the right market. The target is the desired outcome. The strategy is how you are going to get there. You are unlikely to realise the former without the latter.

So perhaps the car dealership needed the very best salesmen in town. People who knew the product inside out. People who could readily empathise and understand what the customer wants. People who could strike exactly the right balance between selling price and maintaining margin. Experienced, brilliant salesmen. A successful car sales business will obviously be about more than just the salesmen, but I pick on that one ingredient to make the point. If the car sales business owner gets those ingredients for success right, success will follow. The targets should look after themselves. The best salesmen produce the best sales results. The targets will be hit *because* the key ingredients of business success are there. But if you ask someone with no sales skills and no product knowledge to hit the same targets they'll be lost at sea. When you ask why are we not hitting our targets it will be tempting to blame the salesman, to start that cycle of frustration; but the more astute business owner might instead first ask whether the ingredients for success are there. Is the business model fit for purpose? That's not to discount the risk – and need to monitor – people not performing in a business from time to time, but we ignore that here because we are purely illustrating that outcomes follow the 'how,' and that merely desired outcomes are not the 'how.'

So if I ever open a coffee shop I will avoid the failure of thinking, simply, 'if I sell 400 coffees a day at £3.75 each, that's about £45k a month.' The 'if' is the part of that sentence to dwell on. What I would need to consider first is *how* I would have a coffee shop deliver those targets. No matter that's what I might *like* the business to do, or what I once saw another coffee shop in London doing. The question for me is *how* is *my* business going to deliver that sort of performance. Answers on a postcard. It might be the best coffee beans in town, the best counter service, the nicest cups, and the greenest footprint, among other things. If the second best in town does 350 cups per day, by being better in all those ways maybe I can hope to sell 400. If I simply leased a shop, employed someone with no interest in coffee or people to front it, served cheap granulated coffee…would those shortcomings be overcome by me walking in and saying to the disinterested front of house staff 'the TARGET is 400 cups per day'? Would that be 'management done'? We all know the answer by now…

TIP

Have a strategy for your business or role achieving its desired outcomes. Merely stating the desired outcomes, without a strategy for getting there, is always to be a day late and a dollar short. Without a strategy – a 'how' – to say *"if I sell x units a day at £x I will make £xxx"* is really just an *"if only"*! If you are not getting the outcomes you desire, consider if anything is missing from the strategy.

****

5

Defensiveness is destructive

Many organisations have created a culture of defensiveness, or have allowed it to enter the organisation by the people who work for it.

Defensiveness often arises from a fear of the consequences of being wrong, or when people think that they are expected to always have the full answer up their sleeve, and can never be wrong. There is perhaps sometimes a strong natural inclination to be defensive, because we fear the shame of failing or being wrong. Being defensive, our subconscious assumes, will guard us against being wrong or from failing – or at least conceal it – so that we might avoid the sense of shame that might follow from failure or being wrong.

Equally, we increasingly in the business community live in an era of respect increasingly for the concept of 'my truth,' which is another way of saying that objective truth no longer exists and that truth is simply whatever you choose to believe it is. If the truth of success and bring right no longer exists, how can you ever fail or be wrong. The subconscious may feel a superficial attractiveness to a strategy that might protect us from the shame of failure or being wrong, but in truth it is a deceit that will not serve us well in business. If the truth for example is that you've let a customer down badly, then telling yourself a lie to avoid the shame of that, in the hope that 'your truth' should get as much respect as anyone else, will just make you look dishonest as well as having failed to perform your role.

Defensiveness can be toxic, because it stifles conversations – or even prevents conversations taking place – that would otherwise create better outcomes for the business.

Consider the two alternative in-person conversations below:

1. The defensive supplier:

Customer:	*"If we ramp up our production numbers, could you increase supply by as much as double?"*
Supplier:	*"Haven't I always delivered whatever you ask?"*
Customer:	*"Yes, I suppose so. We might make another model, bigger than the existing one. Could you provide larger components?"*
Supplier:	*"Don't doubt me. I have told you before: we can do whatever you ask."*
Customer:	*"Ha. Oh, and have you got last month's invoice?"*
Supplier:	*"I asked my secretary to e-mail it to you a week ago; I'll kill her if she hasn't done it already!"*
Customer:	*"Ok, thanks, I'll get going now then, and speak soon."*

2. The non-defensive supplier:

Customer:	*"If we ramp up our production numbers, could you increase supply by as much as double?"*
Supplier:	*"Certainly, our factory is supplying 2 customers and is only at 50% of its current capacity, so that even if we double production for you, we'll still have 25% spare capacity. If needed, we have 2 other factories with similar spare capacity. So we're ready right away. To ensure that stays the case, do let's add this as a reoccurring agenda item; I want to make sure we are always ready to support your next step perfectly, and that we're always a step ahead in being able to provide for your next needs."*
Customer:	*"Great. We might make another model, bigger than the existing one. Could you provide larger components?"*
Supplier:	*"No problem: we already do that for the other customer. We can tool up for any size with 4 weeks' notice."*
Customer:	*"Super, I'll note that and make sure we keep talking for a seamless relationship when the time comes. One last thing - have you got last month's invoice?"*

| Supplier: | *"It should have gone out by e-mail last Monday but as you haven't received it for whatever reason I'd brought a duplicate copy in my bag to today's meeting: here you go."* |
| Customer: | *"Super. Business done! Time for a quick lunch?"* |

Which is the better relationship? The above relationship (in both versions of the conversation) could be a significant one: perhaps one worth £100 million a year. On paper, whichever of the two exchanges took place above, it could from the revenue number alone look like a good situation. In neither of the two alternative conversations did the relationship terminate, at least during the limited illustrative content of the discussions above. But I would say probably only the latter is a genuinely good situation. The former exchange is luke warm at best due to the supplier's defensiveness. The relationship is however guarded and strained because of defensiveness, and is therefore perhaps at risk of an alternative supplier successfully competing for the customer's business, or even for the customer going out and looking for one.

In the former dialogue, the discussion for the customer is a difficult one. A defensive partner is focused on defending themselves, rather than delivering in the manner of a functioning partnership. Such a relationship is unlikely to lead to collaborative thinking leading to improvements for both sides, and is instead likely to be locked in a limited cycle of question and defensive reply. A business relationship characterised by defensiveness on the supplier's side is unlikely to ever be a truly performing one.

Defensiveness makes you difficult to deal with. No customer looks forward to a defensive reply to every interaction. It is trying and wearisome. So that customers might choose not to deal with you. You might think that sounds like an easier life, but it obviously isn't a solid foundation for business success.

The same is true of internal business within a company. We've all been in the situation where we, in a very nice way, ask an employee for something, only to get our heads bitten off by reply: *"Can't you see I'm busy; and didn't I give it to you last week; I've done it already before and you think I haven't; Sarah in the next pod has nothing to do; could she help?"* Such a defensive culture stands in the way of a business functioning well internally because it creates a barrier and stops things from happening.

Defensiveness removes the possibility of improvement. If you are always instinctively and without any analysis defending things as they are, you are probably never going to identify ways to improve. If for example you do a dreadful pitch but in the de-brief that follows get defensive and tell yourself it was a brilliant pitch how are you going to learn from the episode so that your next pitch is better? If you are defending failure or even just mediocrity that is where you will stay.

Defensiveness removes opportunity. Conversations are always killed by a defensive line, and so unlikely to meander into exploring things where opportunity might lie, as illustrated by the two alternative example conversation above. In the second alternative, perhaps the conversation over lunch leads to a new business opportunity…!

The performance of a team can be fundamentally crippled by a culture of defensiveness. Truth and merit become opaque when lies and failure are concealed by defensiveness. Defensive lies might even promote falsehoods or less capable people ahead of truth and real talent. In this way a toxic downward spiral sets in.

Defensiveness probably conceals other bigger problems lurking beneath the surface. If you are too quick to defend all the time, there are probably gremlins the defensiveness is subconsciously covering up. Perhaps you know you are out of your depth, so being defensive in a bid to conceal it. Perhaps you are pathologically closed to the idea of something new, and so defensive of repeating the past. One should usefully see any instinct to act defensively as an indicator of the need to self-appraise: is there a good reason to be defensive, or is it a harmful response?

If the defensive person is trying to avoid criticism, well what customer wants that? If something goes wrong, an acknowledgement or an apology is always better than a defensive cover up, if you have a shred of integrity and if you want the customer to return. If you deal with a business that listens to you and is open-minded you are far more likely to return than to a defensive business.

I have spent many years as a litigation lawyer seeing people expend large sums of money defending the indefensible in Court. It can be so easy, even in litigation and with large sums of money at stake, to only see your side of things, or, to use the ideological words we mentioned above, to see only 'your truth' (because, hey, who is anyone to question 'your truth'). The trouble is if your truth isn't *the* truth, a Court is likely to rule in favour of *the* truth (according to the evidence and law), which means you lose, and lose a lot of money paying not only the damages the other party is entitled to, but all of their costs as well. Whether a tension is just creeping into a dialogue or a relationship or is very advanced, and whether you are facing an issue just rearing its head or all the way deep into litigation, it generally pays to drop the defensive goggles and ask yourself – after considering all perspectives and all the facts and evidence – where the truth and the right outcome lies. Blind defensiveness alone may well cost you your reputation and a lot of money in both lost sales and the consequences of your own blind defensiveness. You'll go down in ignorance of course – being defensive about admitted you have caused your own decline in such a way – but ultimately that won't much sweeten the pill, or change the outcome.

Finally, beware the final danger that defensiveness can become superficially self-affirming in the sense that as defensiveness causes a business harm there becomes more reason to be defensive! In the sense that a naval fleet suffering losses probably needs to increase its defence. But excepting the idea that your business might be suffering physical losses on the battlefield, danger lies down the path of believing that the answer to defensiveness causing a business to decline is yet more defensiveness! No tactically astute navy suffering heavy defeat would defend the idea of continuing down the strategic path that led to those defeats. They would quickly re-appraise and attempt new ideas to arrest the defeat and turn the tide to success instead.

Sometimes a defensive strategy might be right in business, in certain circumstances. But little comes from a defensive culture in the way described above. Remove the defensive culture from your business, and avoid its toxic influence.

TIP

Consciously resist a subconscious tendency to be self-defensive as a mechanism to guard against the risk of shame that might arise from failure or being wrong. Your business will be better able to self-appraise, constantly improve, and your business and business relationships will function better without the resistance that comes about from a culture of being defensive. Realise that defensiveness is a deceit and an empty victory, and that it may cost you customers, money and could even lead to the failure it might have been misguidedly intended to avoid.

****

6

Pedestrian pace

It is of course true that informed decisions are generally better than hurried ones. A rushed decision made without a proper testing or analysis can be one which is regretted later, once there is the luxury of greater time to properly reflect.

However, businesses often take this truth too far and end up positioning their decision-making speed at the opposite end of the spectrum, so that decisions then take too long to make.

A perfect pitch that is only read after another one has already been read and accepted will be too late. I have seen fast movers secure a win despite the existence of a process, which only led the slower movers into a false sense of security that speed is not of the essence. Just because a deadline of 3 months' time is expressed, does not mean you might lose out to a competitor who replies after just 2 weeks, before you get the chance to get around to the submission you had diarised to complete within the 3 months. A quick *and* brilliant response is better than a brilliant but slow response. And do not make the mistake of thinking the decision is always yours and you can decide yes or no at your own pace: the passage of time may take the decision out of your hands.

A thorough 10-stage recruitment process may assist in ensuring the right quality of candidate, assuming the tests achieve that, but at the loss of great hires to alternative faster-moving recruiters. A firm once lost out on hiring a great candidate they wanted purely because its own internal processes just wouldn't be able to move as quickly as a rival offer. The 'loser' comforted itself with the narrative that losing out was better than rushing and failing to follow 'due process.' Not true if that employee would have added value many times her salary, and if a direct competitor now has that added value at the same time as it being your loss.

Do not mistake due diligence (which is usually desirable) with pointless slow speed and needlessly long-drawn-out processes. The former is sometimes used unjustifiably to excuse the latter. There is usually a sweet-spot: due diligence done as quickly as possible, and focusing on what really matters most, and then moving as quickly as possible.

Those who prefer to procrastinate rather than get on with it are usually paralysed by fear of making a decision, or they just aren't sufficiently motivated. Realise the difference between decisions that need time, and ones you delay just because you are afraid of making them. If you aren't sufficiently motivated, work out why and fix it because in that state you can never compete against motivated competitors.

In practice that will be achieved by avoiding management by committee, ie, a structure or process which means too many people have to approve a decision at the cost of any decisions being made quickly.

We saw this above in the context of being quick to secure the best employees. A business that moves at the pace of a London bus will also miss the best sales as well as the best staff. I once spotted a gap in the market for some work which a client's supplier process had not catered for. It was a narrow but attractive line of work which none of the client's suppliers had covered in their tenders and thus there was no formal supplier in place *for that type of work.* Spotting the opportunity, and meeting my contacts within the organisation who confirmed it to be a genuine opportunity, I jumped on preparing a written pitch, demonstrating genuine specialism and experience, and innovative pricing which others could not beat. It then took the organisation I was employed by over 6 months to approve the pitch. By the time it was submitted, other suppliers had also spotted the gap in the market, and already covered it off. The delay had been to ensure that all stakeholders approved the document, and that meant it was too late. There were many months of little tweaks and fettles from a long line of people, on group e-mails which consumed enormous amounts of key senior staff time. Too many cooks spoil the broth. Had the appropriate specialist team and the CEO or other nominated board member had the authority to proceed quickly with an opportunity which was unlikely to exist for a prolonged period, we would have acted quicker and potentially secured a win. Windows of opportunity do not stay open forever. Seize the opportunity when it presents itself. Do not dither while the opportunity passes you by.

It follows that it is enormously beneficial for a business to have a structure and processes that enable it to be nimble, and fast moving. Procurement and other processes have a role, but should be put in place around the need to be nimble, and process should never be allowed to stifle the desire to make things happen when the right opportunity presents itself.

And if the process or delay is in the pursuit of perfectionism realise that perfectionism is often an illusion. One can delay indefinitely in pursuit of perfection. But it is better to act with a nearly perfect product or pitch than be paralysed by the need to keep delaying to make it 'perfect.' Yes, mediocrity is bad and closer to perfect is good, but there is a balance to be struck. Delay in the pursuit of perfectionism will become a self-fulfilling prophecy because as the state of the art in every sector improves over time, the 'perfect' product or service is always changing. And so delaying to chase perfectionism becomes a never-ending hazard. This is something I have to still regularly remind myself.

Some businesses – you may have worked in one – have almost a packed schedule of internal meetings on a daily basis. The idea is that every issue requires a long meeting with a lot of attendees to ensure decisions are properly made. Yes, possibly, in the case of significant issues, but almost certainly not in the case of *every* issue. I've been to meetings where the person who has conduct of the meeting has asked, without joking, *"now what's this meeting about: I'll check outlook."* Such is the inevitable fatigue in a business that schedules too many internal meetings. Do you need a meeting, or would an e-mail or quick call be better? "Let's discuss it face to face!" or "let's pick up the phone and speak," late adopters of e-mail sometimes say. Yes, sometimes a meeting is genuinely required, but know when, and beware of spending your entire day discussing in meetings what could conveniently have been one or two or three short e-mails and 6 hours left spare to achieve other – possibly more significant – things.

Decide what needs to be a meeting, what needs to be a call, and what can conveniently be just an e-mail or message. That's the most efficient way. For example, if I want to decide what day to visit a client, someone in the team might say "*let's jump into a meeting room.*" What would we achieve by an hour later? Instead I could text the client saying 'what day next week to pop in and see you?,' while I wait 5 minutes for the reply I could check everyone's calendar, and when they reply saying 'Tuesday or Thursday any time,' I would know that the whole team can do Thursday and so I reply saying 'see you Thursday at 10:00.' A ten-minute job at most, but if we had an internal meeting or if I phoned everyone, it would take the whole morning.

On the other hand, if a client voiced a complaint or messaged me about something reasonably complex, I'd be the first to suggest a meeting later in the day or first thing in the morning, if the task demanded some face-to-face time because of its importance or complexity. Good judgment, rather than a default process, will probably best serve in deciding how to address a matter.

A similar problem is death by committee: the problem of wanting to discuss everything endlessly among groups of people.

When a new car is designed, having a committee to discuss whether it is ready for sale is probably a good idea. A team input on each of its attributes – style, name, economy, price, and so on – is likely to further refine the product in each area and make it the best it can be.

But it is most certainly not true that the same goes for every minor decision. Should we get the client in to discuss the advice we have sent? Should we book the big conference room for the team meeting? Do you want tea or coffee? These are more likely yes or no answers, and time can only be wasted, and energy zapped, by 'committee-ing' at length, with lots of people involved, every little question that arises.

TIP

Avoid a culture of pedestrian pace, which can kill a business even if it otherwise has the best ideas and products. Imagine if Apple had wanted 100 more meetings to discuss its first generation iPhone before launching to market. It might not yet have reached the market, and Apple might not be the player it is today.

****

7

Death by process

We have already seen how slow decision-making can hold back a business. Worse, it might grind to a halt if a business goes down the route of a slow death by process.

A business had a process of all invoices being issued or amended by a central finance team. The process for staff – even senior staff – interacting with that team was that the team could *not* be contacted individually. The process was that they should be given tasks as a team by the rest of the firm, via computer software, which involved completing the request by way of a number of drop-down or tick-box standard forms, which the team would then process in date order. There were examples of tasks more than 6 months old still to be processed. These were customers screaming *"can I have those overdue fee notes and I'll pay them now."* Only the central team could – and those with the customer relationship couldn't chase because any contact with the team was prohibited! A chaser asking for a fee note requested months before merely ended up in the same queue as the original request, and when they eventually got to it they'd simply respond *"we've done this why are you chasing?"* (I'm not even making that up – a genuine laugh out loud moment). This meant customer expectations being routinely missed because of things taking far too long, and then when they needed to be put right they couldn't be quickly put right by the person – even a senior person – with the relationship. No, instead the dreaded form must be filled out and the process followed. It was like shouting off the top of a mountain and hoping someone in the village below would reply. Nobody knew if or when the reply would come.

And it wasn't as if the process was fit for purpose when it did, after delay, deliver the requested output. A customer once asked the central team for a breakdown of the invoice he had received. The invoice was for about £4,500. The central team responded directly with a breakdown containing one entry for £800,000. The customer then came to the relationship manager in horror – "*this can't be right!*" How could a charge of £4,500 contain a component part worth £800,000? The team was contacted to say this is embarrassing and can we quickly amend the obvious error down the phone came the collective "*tut, tut tut; he's not following the process again.*" They would have to once more fill out the standard electronic form and wait for a miracle. A firm that has terrible processes and is a slave to them might be telling the administrators to fill in a form when they realise they've choked their own enterprise to its deathbed.

As if the invoicing process was not bad enough, the same applied to IT. An IT query, request or problem meant e-mailing a generic IT e-mail address, waiting for a ticket with a number on, and expect a response in date order. And a slap on the wrist for the key man in a client meeting needing a non-responsive projector urgently switching on for a presentation due to start *right this minute*. He's not following the process again! Take a ticket and stand in line, you moron! Arrgh! Would it be better if people could phone finance or IT and have a person fix the problem there and then? No, take a ticket and stand in line. The process is bigger than us all.

I've seen the same thing in the NHS. Phone 111 to get advice on a skin burn and they'll tell you to stop getting quite so quickly to the point, thank you very much caller! No, you must follow the process. There will be 50 questions first. Have you got tingling in the arms? No. Any chest pain? No. And on it goes. After 50 'nos' and half an hour later the operative then wants to know why the heck you are calling. Er, as I tried to explain when you first answered the phone – just a quick bit of advice on a skin burn. And whether you are operating to maximise profit or serve the taxpaying public, wasted time due to pointless process is not good. I once stood in A&E for an age to then answer 20 questions the triage nurse seemed to be trained to ask by the computer screen, to be told to go home and the appropriate doctor would call. Nobody ever did. But to the manager in charge who put process ahead of outcomes and service, all is probably well because the process had always been followed.

I have seen a recruitment process that was all about generic scoring rather than the substance of the candidates' answers. Seemingly arising from the need to eliminate judgement and have everything down to a process. When probably more judgement than process was needed. Let's imagine the first assessment question was 'explain a time when you learned something' and points were awarded for (i) observation (ii) listening (iii) analysis and (iv) learning (a 25% score for demonstrating each skill with a total available score of 100%). A candidate who gives the example of opening the front door to the postman, *observing* he seemingly wants to chat about something, *listening* to him saying I couldn't find your door number, *analysing* that the door number is rusty and barely visible, and *learning* to order a new door number the same morning, would score a 100%, as all 4 skills deemed worthy of a score by the process are demonstrated. Whereas a candidate who says they suspected the government was losing £500 million a year, approached a senior Cabinet Minister to propose a method to recoup that, piloted a scheme and put that sum back into the public purse, would score nothing for observation and as this was a lead based on speculation instead, nothing for listening as it is all about talking, a point for analysis and none for learning as there is no lesson. A score of just 25%. I think we as human beings can analyse the better example and who we might recruit. But a dull recruitment process hung up on a bland score sheet rather than looking at the substance of answers produced poor results. It would recruit people talking about opening a front door above people with amazing experience and stories to tell. Beware. Sometimes decisions and actions require good judgement. Rather than simply a process. Do not make the mistake of thinking a blind process is a substitute for good judgement exercised by the right people.

And a process mentality ahead of judgement-led thinking can lead down some awful rabbit holes. I remember some insurance claims handlers having fraud checklists based on historic fraud data. The idea was that the data underlying past frauds would help spot future frauds. So anyone called Kevin from Bradford with a BMW and who had chased a reply to his claim more than once a month was red flagged for investigation for fraud. And he would receive an email from someone with 'fraud' in their job title on their e-mail sign off. Even though more likely than not he had committed no fraud. Put yourself in that man's shoes. Delay, and then an email from the fraud squad, in reply to your perfectly honest claim. He isn't likely to renew. Process running the show usually means a lot of questionable outcomes and customer service to make you cringe.

Beware the trap of thinking the answer to business is inventing a process for every little thing, which might just instead slow everything down, prevent delivery, eliminate the opportunity for good judgement and cause harm, and cost a fortune in wasted management time frustrated by, and in compensating for, the consequences of over-process.

TIP

Processes are to facilitate things happening in a business. If the process becomes king, rather than the outcome to process should facilitate, you are entering the realms of death by process. The tail wagging the dog. Reign it in, and stay focused on judgement and outcomes above process, before process strangles you.

✶✶

8

One size fits all

A sister problem to the risk of 'death by process' is the mistake of thinking one size fits all.

Indeed, once a process is devised it is tempting to think that in order to get value from that process it must be adopted by all. No exceptions. No excuses. I witnessed this in law firms. So that operations managers could monitor trends and data across the business, they would design a form which everyone would be asked to complete when, for example, taking on a new instruction from a client. Data fields would be compulsory. Commercial litigators would be asked to enter 'personal injury type' (when there was none), and commercial advisors would be asked to enter an 'accident date' (when there was none), just because a percentage of the firm happened to do personal injury claims. A one-size-fits-all mentality meant the completing irrelevant fields – or having discussions over why they were left unpopulated – was a waste of time for those to whom such fields had no application.

It went beyond data. I remember operations managers and internal auditors demanding that I make a team of lawyers waste half an hour every time they opened a new case by completing an initial 'case plan.' This was something observed by injury lawyers dealing with simple cases on an outsourced or 'delegated authority' model so that there was some evidence (in the absence of advices to and instructions from clients) of what they intended to do and achieve on the case. However that was redundant on the cases my lawyers were handling because we prepared detailed advices to clients and then recorded the client's instructions in meeting or telephone notes, so that a case plan on the front cover of the file merely duplicated what already existed elsewhere. Clients did not demand a 'case plan' and would not even know about one if it was there. It was a waste of time and money. But to the one-size-fits-all manager, we could not be an exception to the one-size-fits-all rule and we must waste half an hour on each case on an exercise which added nothing and had no value.

Some companies have a central chart showing salary bands by years of experience or grade. And nobody can be paid more. Computer says no. But what about those employees who might do more than their job description, and justify a higher salary? One size does not fit all, and such businesses often struggle to retain high performing junior employees. A chart stating salary bands based on experience or grade was probably born of a desire to ensure a fair approach across the business. But if all that does is under-reward people going above and beyond the regular job description, will a perception of fairness compensate for losing those people. If there needed to be a chart, a one-size-for-all approach, it probably needs to be far more complex and less rigid to allow scope to accommodate special cases.

Decisions appropriate to particular circumstance, are usually preferable to one-size-fits-all. There is a reason, for example, why BMW group operates different showrooms with different ways of working for their Mini, BMW and Rolls Royce brands. Or VW group across its Skoda, VW and Audi brands. The different sectors require different types of service. At the Skoda end of the market, for example, it may be that the volume of sales and margin on sales might dictate that time available to each customer has a certain limitation. At the Rolls Royce end it may be that customers are given more individual attention without time constraint and or any hint of one-size-fits-all. Don't be deceived by thinking that one-size-fits-all is somehow the prize of 'consistency' or seduced by the easiness of treating everything in the same way. Bespoke rivals very often deliver very much better to their markets – and secure more business – than a one-size-fits-all competitor which – purely for the convenience, laziness or imagined 'consistency' of its internal set up – failed to properly focus itself to the market. Imagine if BMW Group decided to centralise the client journey across its brands. Mini Cooper (around £23,000) buyers would experience an identical journey to Rolls Royce La Rose Noire Droptail (around £32 million) customers. Whoever comes up with the central process may boast of savings in complexity, effort and cost of having multiple processes. But I think we can all reliably guess the adverse financial impact at the front line would be vastly greater.

The 8th best-selling car and best-selling 'supermini' class car in the UK in 2023 is the Mini. It is easily the smallest car in the top 10. The others are larger SUVs or class-above hatches. It outsold cheaper rivals like the Vauxhall Corsa, Toyota Yaris and VW Polo. The Mini is famously customisable in terms of trim which makes its buyers feel unique and special. A sort of 'budget' Rolls Royce. While Ford announced this year an intention to discontinue its Fiesta model, Mini sold over 210,000 units in the first 3 quarters of 2023. And the average selling price of a Mini, fuelled by the options list, is higher than its less customisable rivals. By recognising that one size does not fit all, Mini has proven that you can be a best seller in a market even when you are not the cheapest price.

It is always tempting to fall for the superficial 'saving' in time and / or cost of a one-size-fits-all process. If BMW Group for example ditched its Mini and Rolls Royce showrooms and staff, and sold all models through BMW dealerships, that move of itself would no doubt be a saving of many £ millions. Superficially, whichever manager made that change could claim a hefty bonus for saving big bucks from the cost column of the accounts by 'simplifying' process. But we all know this would hit sales and profits by taking away the bespoke customer-focused journey possible by separating the brands. And likely be more than any saving associated by a one-size-fits-all approach, which is why the business does not do it. Occasionally there may be times where a one-size-fits-all approach could yield dividends, but surrendering a business to a pervading culture of one-size-fits-all is likely to be a mistake, and one must always carefully count the true cost (down the line as well as immediate impact).

TIP

It can be tempting in the name of simplicity to think that one size fits all. But one size rarely does fit all. Simplicity is no prize if it trashes the greater prize of success from respecting that different markets, and even different customer within markets, want different things. The most successful businesses try to focus on delivering for the customer, and recognising that customer's wants and needs as individual. The success that comes from so doing is usually higher than any more modest saving of time and cost by centralising processes to a one-size-fits-all model.

****

9

A lack of self-awareness

In chapter 3 we explored the difference between racing drivers Alain Prost and the late Ayrton Senna. The real lesson there may be one of self-awareness: in realising your position in any market and being aware of your customers and their needs. Prost and Senna would have been able to wax lyrical about why they took such different approaches to their sport. And both would have, in their own ways, demonstrated a high level of self-awareness and awareness of the competition. And both achieved a deserved high level of success. The only sure route to failure is a lack of analysis and awareness: not to know where you are on, in what we called in chapter 3, the mathematician / star-gazer-o-meter, or not to know your customers or competition. To be Prost and not know why you are slowing down once the lead is achieved. Or to be Senna and not know why your foot is still hard on the gas already with a long lead. Or not knowing what the other is doing, or why. Properly appraise your product or service, your market position, your customers, and feel assured in the deliberate position that leads you to adopt. Avoid being vulnerable for just blindly 'being,' or coasting, without knowing why. We remember Prost and Senna for their brilliant – if different – strategies. We (and the record books) have long forgotten the drivers who coasted obliviously somewhere in between.

In my own profession, law, I have known some brilliant lawyers who too often doubt themselves. I'm not saying that being humble isn't better than being full of empty pride, but brilliant advice that doubts itself unduly can cause the listener to start to doubt it too (even if it is brilliant advice) and thus the brilliant advice is diminished in some way. Equally, I have known plenty of pretty poor lawyers with a blind arrogance that leads them never to question themselves, or to look for opportunities for self-development and growth. That leads them to make mistakes of judgement, and be judged poorly by clients in the longer-term, and for them to then not to even realise it when it happens, or if the client complains so loudly that they cannot fail to realise something is going on, they will blame the client, or someone else, which in the eye of the intelligent observer just diminishes them even more. The point is that a touch more self-awareness would help both categories of person. The brilliant but doubting lawyer might grow slightly in confidence through a little more self-awareness, and be better for it, in the sense of less doubt causing less delay, and more confidence adding a much appropriate air of authority to the right advice. Equally, the poor but ignorant person might through more self-awareness gain a much-needed opportunity for learning and self-correction.

To perform in business one needs to analyse the strengths, weakness, opportunities and threats of the business within its chosen market. This takes more self-awareness than some businesses have. Every business boasts that it is brilliant. But I'm sure we can all – even the most tolerance among us – identify some businesses which claim to be brilliant but which are very much not. We've all seen a business claiming to be "*the best in town*" but which is in truth more like the worst in the world. But it's often not just the sales pitch which is out of alignment with reality. It is very much worse: it is the awareness of itself. I once saw a tiler put tiles on a wall in a way they were not aligned. Rather than a straight line across the wall between each row, there were 'steps' between each row so that the tiles were not in a perfect grid but slightly all over the place.

It was, by any objective standard, a diabolical job. But he seemed genuinely to think it was good. Now the problem for this business was not that its work was dire. Which was going to lead to non-payment, call backs, and possibly litigation. But that it thought its work was good when it was bad. That leads to being locked into disappointing customers, being surprised when they are disappointed, and then frustrated by the ensuing battles over whether the work was good enough. Now this is an extreme and obvious example. But in more subtle ways your business might lack self-awareness and it might be holding it back. Businesses are run by people and it is human nature – a survival instinct – to over-estimate your own strengths, and under-recognise the weaknesses. It takes a lot to dig deep and be properly self-aware. To see your business as its harshest critic might. And far from 'talking the business down,' that is where you will see your biggest opportunities for improvement, and the rewards which that will bring.

What is needed at all times in business is the constant reality check. By which I mean benchmarking against client expectations, rigorous audits of quality and outcomes, checking the competition and remaining competitive, and ensuring the basic financial viability, ie, that the income exceeds the costs. Ignore those things through arrogance or ignorance and think that the regular churn and the status quo is a success story at your peril.

TIP

Pride comes before a fall. Not seeing clearly every aspect of your business leads to failing to grasp the full picture. Be self-aware and enjoy the double advantage of avoiding the pitfalls of a lack of self-awareness, and of getting ahead of less conscious rivals.

****

10

Continuous improvement

Businesses either embrace or reject the concept of constant improvement. World class businesses embrace it. World class businesses wake up each day asking how they can be better today than they were yesterday. Average businesses coast along repeating each day in much the same way as yesterday. A Rolls Royce is not a brilliant motor car by accident, Apple products are not leading in the tech sector by accident, James Dyson's vacuum cleaners are not the best by accident. Those organisations are constantly looking for scope to improve. They don't think 'we are the best' in the sense of the complacency that brings. Nor do they see an improvement as a criticism of yesterday's product. There is a culture of continuous improvement.

Businesses that reject a culture of constant improvement instead have a mistaken culture of believing that improvement is somehow mocking the status quo. *"What's wrong with how we do things now?,"* such a business might ask. A leader in such a business might say something like *"things aren't bad as they are."* They see an idea to be better as an insult to the present. There may be egos in the room mistaking continuous improvement for criticism of what they have created, ie, how things are right now. The better business leader will put his ego aside, be emotionally mature enough to know that a culture of continuous improvement is better for the business and its people than some kind of inertia based on a misplaced sense of ego.

Alternatively the stuck-in-a-rut business might be led by laziness rather than the ego barrier. You can see that in companies like Woolworths that failed just by failing to keep up with the times. At the risk of being unkind and exaggerating to make a point, it looked a bit the same when it failed as it did 20 years earlier. It did not look like a business trying to always be better. The pick and mix was stocked at front of house. The top 40 CDs were on the shelf at the back. Job done. If the competition was opening bespoke sweet shops with a far wider range and better quality, so what. If CDs were going west in favour of streaming, look the other way. But business as usual without continuous improvement one day becomes business behind the curve; business made redundant.

It is far better to buy into the idea that anything and everything can be always be better. Once you accept that as your baseline principle, you can embrace the rewards of it being your goal to continuously find ways to be better.

A business that improves itself by just 1% per day will be over 250% times better in just one year than a business that instead stands still, that believes that it is already 'good enough.'

In the motor sector, for example, the best car manufacturing brands are always looking for ways to improve. Even between new model launches, existing models will be tweaked where opportunities to do so are identified. When LED headlamps came of age for example and were better than xenon, the continuous improvement manufacturer will update the specification of existing and not just future models, to ensure their products remain the best they can be.

Apple can sometimes be teased by some observers for their grand announcement of their endless incremental improvements. Each iteration being 20% faster than the last model, or with a screen 10% brighter, may not seem earth-shattering by itself, but compare the current iPhone to the launch model and you can see where a culture of constant improvement takes you.

TIP

A culture of continuous improvement is your friend not your enemy. Overcome inertia or ego and reap the rewards that come with incessant improvement.

****

11

That's the way we've always done it: resistance to change

"That's the way we've always done it." The words of a militant secretary completely incapable of flexibility or embracing change. Or the words of the out-of-his-depth manager who sees change as a threat to the comfort blanket of the old familiar ways. Or the naïve entrepreneur who thinks that repeating the ways of a successful past must inevitably produce success in the future, neglecting to note that times and markets change.

Whoever it may be who utters such words, allowing them to dictate the business culture will ensure that any business is held back.

Almost certainly the best of the competition will be continually scanning for changes or innovations which might allow them to provide better service or a better product, or achieve efficiencies meaning more competitive prices or additional cash for research and development, or other investment in the business.

To return to motor industry innovation, some failed British manufacturers were slow to fully embrace automation in production, out of some misplaced idea that a man with a hammer was better than a precision laser-guided robot, and as a result fell behind in build standards and quality and long term cost efficiencies.

In professional services, those who thought buying their employees laptops and smart phones – dismissing it as an unnecessary cost – were penalised in failing to gain from employees inevitably working longer hours flexibly by, for example, dealing with an e-mail which comes in at 20:00 at night, or taking a client video call while commuting to the office at 08:00. The technology pays for itself and then some. To shy away from it by focusing on the up-front cost alone, and failing to recognise changing ways of working – away from as well as in the office – and the client demand for that and the extra revenue it produces if embraced, was to miss a trick and fall behind.

Ocado, the online supermarket, has and continues to invest huge sums in grocery home delivery. There was a time – and it perhaps still exists to some extent – where consumers preferred to visit a supermarket and select their own groceries, for freshness, inspiration or whatever. But slick distribution can deliver goods fresh as those you'd find on the shelf (if not fresher – as their journey is shorter) and a slick app or website can rival the inspiration you'd experience in store. As the drawbacks of online grocery shopping become fewer, the advantages such as the time saving might tip more and more people into thinking it beats visiting a physical store. It might still be a relatively small section of the overall market, but I think Ocado is right to be looking at what grocery shopping might increasingly look like in the future.

Those afraid of embracing change see only the risks, or cling onto the past out of some sense of nostalgia. They see false security in the status quo. Why take a risk when we're doing fine as we are, is a question I have often heard and which has, without scrutiny, superficial force. But the reality is that there is no security in the status quo. No decision or stance is without risk, even the status quo. At its extreme, the change and risk averse business owner could see his business collapse around him, by fearing to make or embrace the changes and risks that are necessary – and which his competitors take – to succeed in the future. This is a particular risk in sectors which have, in the recent past, been slow to change or take risks, because recent experience will have 'proven' in an imagined not real sense in the minds of the cautious the perceived security in the status quo. The more balanced, and likely more successful business, will consider against the risk of change the risk of doing nothing. And it is by no means certain that in every situation the greater risk is the former.

Markets change. Sometimes quickly. Sometimes slowly. But it is near-certain that change will occur. Those who anticipate and prepare for it will win. Those who embrace it when it happens may survive. Those who fail to anticipate it or embrace it when it comes will likely fail.

The Board of Woolworths was probably in its dying days having shop floor meetings saying why can't we repeat the glory days. We are doing everything the same. But it might have been just that – staying stuck and not changing while the rest of the sector did – that brought about the end.

Look at the once dominant Blackberry and its failure to adapt to the mobile device market moving to touch screen technology without buttons or keyboards. Its Board might well have thought, while everyone switched to iPhones and Samsungs, how can we be losing market share when our products are as good as they ever were. Well yes, but if a preferred technology emerges an old one might lose favour.

Staying the same, resisting change, will usually fail because markets and times change. Those who anticipate and embrace it will be the next winners.

Staying in your comfort zone and just being on repeat is likely to lead you to fail to see, and even less to adapt to, changing markets.

TIP

'This is the way we've always done it' is not, of itself, a reason to keep doing it the same way. Inevitably changing times and evolving markets are more likely to be a reason not to stay the same. A focus on the best approach, for the moment, and for the future, will produce better results than naively thinking that repeating the past in different times will produce the same results, or lazily or nostalgically clinging to past ways for their own sake.

---

* *

12

A culture of talent and merit

So many businesses have an applaudable desire to treat everyone fairly. But some misunderstand the concept of fairness and instead of achieving a culture of true fairness they instead pursue uniformity, perhaps because they confuse the two things.

We hear so much these days, for example, about equality of pay for employees. Everyone in the same role we are told must be paid exactly the same. Why should a male salesman be paid more than his female colleague? We must all be treated equally, it is said. They would have the female colleague paid exactly the same as her male colleague. But is that necessarily the fair outcome? If a lady salesman sold ten products each day on average, whereas her male colleague achieved only five daily average sales, should we not pay the lady twice what her male colleague earns? To pay her only the same would be unfair. She is working harder and being more successful. The fair outcome is to reward her for that. They might be in the same role, but it would be grossly unfair to pay them the same, because one is earning a right to be paid more than the other. In this way uniformity can be very *un*fair. And so it is that we must avoid a plea for fairness lapsing into a culture of turgid uniformity where there is no incentive to ever go the extra mile, because everyone is treated the same regardless of how well they perform. Once such a culture takes hold, it can drain the life from any business by deterring effort and rewarding the opposite.

Equally, if a photocopying clerk on his first day in a company reads a document and suggests a way for the business to earn £1m in additional sales, then it would be foolish for his entrepreneurship to be hampered by a business that only promotes internally to sales after 4 years' service. A good business would fully embrace his talents by moving him into a role where they can make an impact, to maximise the outcome for the employee and the business. Treating people fairly truly means treating them based on their contribution, and regardless of their background, gender, race, religion or otherwise. Only when you embrace that have you got a true culture of fairness.

One of the number one complaints I hear from employees is that they are working all the hours God sends *just to make someone else rich*. At its simplest level, they do of course have a point. After all, that is the employment model. The employees earn a reasonable salary for doing the work. And the owners share in the reward. Whether a business makes £1m or £100m in a year, the employees, or at least most of them, probably earn the same salary either way. The owners, on the other hand, will take a share in the increased profitability. Even if it is the work of the employees, rather than the owners, that resulted in the increased profitability.

What this often does is create a 'them and us' culture. Employees grumble that they toil away only for someone else's reward. Once such a culture sets in, it is a catalyst for complacency and surrender. It will not only cause employees to work less hard, and contribute less, but ultimately impact on the profits and thus the reward of the owners.

Much better than a 'them and us' culture is a 'we all rise together' culture. Not because of some mis-placed desire for blanket equality of outcome – on the contrary, we have railed against just that above – but because if everyone feels part of the success, and shares fairly in the reward, the success will be far more sustainable, and ultimately greater.

This is not to say that the receptionist should get paid as much as the CEO. But if the CEO one year earns £5m on the back of the company's success, and a middle manager who brought in five new major client accounts that contributed to that success gets told he can't have a salary rise from £60k, you can imagine how the middle manager might not be as motivated to work quite so hard next year. Indeed, the middle manager might well give up and simply maintain his five client accounts rather than spending the extra energy on bagging another five, for fear of that going unrewarded again. After all, people make sacrifice for work in terms of family, health, time, opportunity cost and so on, and they'll only do that if they feel like it is worth it. Dare I say a sensible CEO might have taken £4.5m instead of £5m, and given out the £500k to his top performers in pay rises and bonuses. That might well contribute to an even stronger performance and make the CEO £6m the following year, whereas an owner who keeps it all for himself instead risks a demotivated key workforce, and a collapse in reward the following year.

The problem can be especially acute in business where the top brass fear recruiting talent as a threat to themselves. That can lead to heavy recruitment at an average and / or junior grade, and a big gap between the people in charge and everyone else. The junior people will get frustrated that they are 'kept down' to avoid them getting close to the bosses. It is usually better to recruit the best talent one can find, and to see the benefit to that to the business as a whole, rather than from the individual political angle of younger talent being a perceived threat to the senior old guard. Such a perception is a highly individualistic one rather than looking instead at the strength of the wider team, and should probably disqualify one from high office in a good business. Imagine the business where the owner earns £500k from a business with five other employees who each earn £25k. No recruitment happens between those two extremes, because the owner perceives capable or more senior people as threat to himself. But if he took the plunge and recruited some real performers on £150k each, maybe his own earnings could go from £500k to £1m, if he embraced those performers introducing changes or improvements to increase the income of the business as a whole. A rising tide lifts all boats.

A business where politics dictates everything can also stifle performance. If mediocre or bad people get into a management position, and surround themselves with other mediocre or bad people they are chums with, or who flatter them, or who represent no 'threat,' a business can quickly become repugnant to anyone with real talent, with the outcome that your business will be bad or mediocre at best, and the talent will join your competitors. Be sure that your business is recruiting, promoting and treating its people based on talent and performance. If back slapping and politics take the place of more objective and wholesome yardsticks, you aren't winning by having a 'loyal' and eager-to-please team around you: instead your loss is those are the only people who will surround you.

TIP

Your business and its results will be as good as your people. Don't think that paying people highly is bleeding your profits: if you get the right people they are what makes your profits (greater). Leave ego, politics and individualism at the door and recruit and promote on the basis of talent and performance, for the benefit of the business and everyone in it. Share the reward or else pay the bigger price of a morale crash and brain drain caused when employees see reward shared unfairly.

****

13

Short-termism

One can have short and long-term goals in a business which is here for the long term. One cannot have (successful) long-term goals in a business which exists only for the short-term. Indeed, if a business is targeting survival and success in the long rather than just the short term, it will need to beware influences which run against that by being short term.

We have all seen, for example, businesses that take external private equity or other investment where the investor has a very short term – perhaps 2 or 3 year – target to double its money. That if not constrained could lead to the dominance of a mere *"money today"* culture, where all that matters is cash today. What is wrong with cash today? Nothing, of itself. But it can be a problem if it is at the expense of cash tomorrow.

If one focuses too much on profit, at the cost of losing focus on other things, it risks distracting one from the real things *that will produce a profit*. The best businesses have a passion for doing something, and because they execute the idea well, it makes money. The best businesses will generate a profit from their activities. The focus will be on those activities, rather than profit itself.

I have seen lawyers, for example, who take a transactional job, perhaps the purchase of a property, and see it purely as a way to bill a load in fees this month, perhaps to allow them to hit target for their own bonus pot, but at the expense of making the client feel like an over-charged cash-cow and with the consequence the client goes elsewhere for his next 100 jobs. The better legal business would focus on being brilliant at transactional services, and would make good profit in a sustainable long term way from that ongoing activity.

Apple for example focuses on producing the next brilliant Macbook or iPhone, or even a new product entirely, as opposed to waking up and crudely thinking 'let's double the price of Macbook to double our profits.' No, doing that might kill sales. Nor do they think let's halve the number of staff in Apple stores. No, bad service would kill a major reason why people buy Apple. Instead the business focuses on producing great products and giving great service.

Dyson too focuses on producing the best vacuum cleaner in the market, and other products. It doesn't wake up and think oh we can halve the power of our cleaners and save money and boost profits. Yes, in theory a cost saving might boost the profit figure on a spreadsheet. But the superior cleaning power of the product is the reason it outsells the competition, and before long word of the impact of such cost saving on the performance of the product would cause sales to nosedive, and would reduce rather than increasing profits.

In professional services, if the only objective each day is to maximise profit that might prompt the activities below, with the unfortunate effects outlined alongside:

Activity	Short term effect which the profiteering CEO will focus on	Wider and longer-term effects which the cash-hungry CEO may be blind to and which may, ultimately, undermine the business
Raise the hourly rates charged to clients to the highest rate possible.	A sudden boost in cash generated by each hour worked.	• Clients looking elsewhere for more competitive rates • Clients demanding more because people expect a very high level of service for a high price • The business being incapable of suddenly aligning its quality with the raised price

		(for example, if Kia suddenly raised its prices to those charged by Porsche, would the product or service match the price?) • Employees demanding greater reward as they see their own value to the business increase • Rival businesses seeing an opportunity to undercut to steal all the work, but still make a return.
Bleed every case for all it is worth, by spending as many hours as possible on it.	A sudden boost in revenue per case.	Clients feeling ripped off, and going elsewhere.
Demanding payment up front, or on much shorter payment terms than before.	A business that doesn't wait to turn effort into cash.	Clients moving elsewhere, to be able to pay when the work is done and on more sane payment terms.
Starting to charge for lots of extras on top of the basic price, such as an admin fee for copying, billing, printing, etc.	A new an extra revenue stream.	Clients feeling squeezed for every penny, and asking are they paying for every overhead of their supplier on top of the price, and going elsewhere to avoid that.
The cutting of costs such as employee salaries or support staff, blaming a tough market or other external factors, or even a downturn in work volume (possibly caused by the above steps).	A business that is lean and mean.	• Employee demotivation, causing • Productivity in decline • Profit-making workers making less due to having to pick up support functions themselves, rather than by lower-cost support staff, causing reduced rather than increased profit.

A focus on employee activity being only those things that directly and immediately produce profit, such as ten hour days working at desks on only fee-making work.	A 33% increase in turnover in the first month of making this change.	<ul><li>Burnout</li><li>No activity on future marketing</li><li>No activity on client relationship management and development (possibly at greater cost than the short-term increase in turnover).</li></ul>

A management consultant charged with lifting profits by a third might be attracted to recommending the steps in column 2 above. On a basic spreadsheet one could demonstrate how those steps might in an abstract world indeed lift profits. But in the real world the consequences would instead be those in the final column, and profits would at least beyond the immediate short term, nosedive instead of rising.

Levi is a good example of a company that got brave enough to tell its investors directly that it intended to manage its business for the long-term and not provide quarterly earnings reports. Investors liked it. Are perhaps even investors (or some of them at least) becoming wise to the fact that everything geared towards nothing but a fast return by profit maximisation might, ironically, be self-defeating? Despite a strong management desire to always do the right thing, through a stated objective of *"profits through principles,"* and to run the business for the long not the short term – or perhaps because of that – annual net income at Levi rose from $135m to $395m.

Suppliers too might also be treated differently in a business focused only on the short term. Why develop a relationship and treat people properly if you are only interested in maximising revenue for a very short period and then exiting? This may lead suppliers to put you down their list of priorities, offer you less favourable terms and charge more.

A lack of investment may also be a symptom of a short-term business model. Why invest for results 3 years down the line if you aren't planning on being around in 3 years? Let's say you are running a café which has been so successful online selling high quality pantry staples that you really need a warehouse and shipping operation, because servicing the online sales from the back office at the café has hit maximum capacity and is holding growth back. If you can see the investment costing £500k but credibly and cautiously accelerating annual sales from £250k today to £500k in 2 years, the investment might look like a no-brainer. Indeed, the investment covers itself in 2 years, and thereafter has boosted revenue by 100%. If you were targeting an exit in 2 years however, you would view the investment as a nil return, rather than a 100% boost, simply by viewing the business through a time-limited window of operation.

Employees can become demoralised in a short-term business, where everything becomes about this financial quarter's results. Staff can feel robbed of the freedom to creatively improve the business, because everyone in the organisation is being pushed to only focus on a very short-term number. Paradoxically, forcing everyone to focus on delivering a short-term number can mis-direct resource away from alternative activity which might, in a slightly longer timescale, produce very much better results. A business focused on increasing revenue by 15% in the current quarter, for example, might put its sales people on part time hours, or re-deploy them to making the product or delivering the service the business sells. That saving or re-deployment of effort might in the current quarter help with increasing revenue, but the same business will almost certainly then complain in the following quarter that the sales pipeline looks too light, with the consequent dip in revenue in the following period.

Ironically, short termism can lead to worse outcomes even in the short term. It can throttle a business in the longer term. It is human nature to want success quickly, and to be in a hurry, and sometimes a short-term approach might be genuine (let's say for example in a sector where for whatever reason demand is dying), but one should be on guard for self-defeating actions caused by a focus only on the immediate term.

TIP

Unless you have a short-term strategy for particular reasons, beware the negative impact of short-termism on business. A short-term strategy will usually compromise long-term success. Businesses exist of course to make a profit. But beware that a move that superficially looks likely to increase profit might because of other factors do the very opposite. The answer is to analyse more broadly than just thinking one move can win a game of chess.

****

14

Failure

Some businesses lack the courage or self-belief to prepare for success. Instead they gear up to the worst-case-scenario. So if they win a big customer, they'll stay focused on the 'what if we lose them' position. They'll under-resource in the belief that if they lose the new customer they won't want surplus staff. They'll under-invest in plant in case it isn't needed in a year's time. They'll not invest in the technologies that might fuel a more successful tomorrow, because what if tomorrow isn't successful. The trouble is that such a cautious philosophy often becomes self-fulfilling: the customer can tell when their business is being under-resourced, and it'll be the reason the customer does end up looking elsewhere instead. And the lack of investment in plant and technologies will lead to a competitive disadvantage against those rivals who do so invest.

The potential double hazard for the over-cautious business is they'll see the customer's departure or the mediocre future results as vindication of their cautiousness. 'Ah-ha!,' the over-cautious business owner will say, 'thank goodness I didn't recruit more staff and thank goodness I didn't invest in future plant and technologies, because we wouldn't be able to afford it now!' But the real question, which goes unasked, is whether it was the failure to invest that itself led to the failure.

This is not to say throw money away, or direct investment in the wrong things, but embracing opportunity and resourcing it properly is generally the way to thrive in business. Hiring the staff to delight your customers is probably a way to retain those customers, and to go and get more. Failing to hire enough staff to delight your customers is probably a way to lose them, and earn a reputation that may make finding more a challenge. Buying the factory needed to achieve the next level of volume is probably what will drive your business forwards to a new level of success. Failing to invest in the factory needed to win big orders will probably be the way to ensure you don't win the big orders. Under-resourcing, or being overly cautious is usually to bring about failure.

Businesses that plan to fail, by their own failure to invest by fearing failure, often mistakenly believe their own caution is guarding against future risk. So a business that runs everything in a threadbare way might convince itself that caution is appropriate because there could in the future be a downturn in business. But as we have seen, resourcing and planning for failure will often lead to failure. If you've underperformed during the good times, because of a caution born of future potential risk, ironically the consequential muted performance during the good times won't help during the bad times. The more correct view is a more nuanced one: make hay while the sun shines, and at the same time have a plan for the risks that may strike.

The true way to guard against risk is to plan for it. The late great Michael Crichton's fictional story in Jurassic Park, made into a movie which grossed over $1 billion, was one of a failure to prepare for the worst. When the storm knocked the power out on an island which was a tourist attraction with dinosaurs in pens, down came the electric fences that kept the dinosaurs away from the human visitors to the park, with death and catastrophe the result. However spectacular the business, and Jurassic Park the fictional enterprise was a story unrivalled in innovation, scale and wonder, invest in a plan for when things don't always go to plan. A backup system might have kept T Rex in his pen. Keep your Velociraptor at bay with a plan B.

While dinosaurs on earth seem like a remote risk to business and humanity today, asteroid strike further pandemic, volcanic activity, increasingly sophisticated crime, war and terrorism provide examples of possible next catastrophes that will catch out the unprepared if and when they strike.

Some businesses had utterly failed to prepare for the recent coronavirus. Very little disaster-proofing had been done in some businesses. There was no disaster management plan. True planning for the bad times involves investing in a strategy to handle those times, and simply being over-cautious about running the business properly in the good times will not only fail to help in the good times it will probably be no help in the challenging times either. The best hospitality businesses, especially food, very quickly pivoted during the pandemic to take away or home delivery orders. And the very best found themselves making more money than before the pandemic. These were generally the 'go-getter' players in their trade even before the pandemic. They invested in leading menus, top chefs, premises, being on-trend, seasonal, sustainable and all that to maximise revenues in the good times, and they threw themselves at an alternative plan b during the pandemic. Food businesses that were limping along with stale models before the pandemic were the ones to give up and close down during the pandemic. It was the ambitious players, not the cautious ones, that best survived adversity. Probably because the ambition and ingenuity that drives maximised performance in the good times is what will provide the resilience and adaptability in the more challenging times.

Moreover, some businesses went into a state of entire paralysis in response to the coronavirus pandemic, refusing to take any key decisions or spend any money. They ended up ceding advantage to rivals who continued to seize opportunity, in terms of bagging the best people and clients and opportunities. A Financial Times survey suggested only 15% of businesses were hiring as planned before the pandemic, or more, and one wonders if they gained a huge advantage by having the choice of the best candidates that would usually be spread across the whole market, and at a time when, because of lay-offs elsewhere, more talent was searching. If you can, find a way through a situation and see any advantages to it, rather than simply ceasing all action due to fear.

A strategy of failure may not sound like the best idea in business. But a tolerance of the risk of failure is an essential part of business success. If you see too much risk in any gamble, you are unlikely to be significantly successful.

James Dyson, for example, recently revealed he has spent as much as £500m developing an electric car, but then abandoned the project completely for reasons of economic viability.

For a famous vacuum cleaner and other gadget manufacturer to try to compete in the busy automotive sector would, to many, have seemed like an awful risk. We've seen how Tesla took a relatively long time to make a profit, and how the established big motor manufacturers are now quickly catching up and producing a range of electric cars.

Unsurprisingly Dyson's car has a number of innovations. Lithium ion batteries with a claimed real-world range of 600 miles from a large 7 seater SUV, special economic and comfortable tyres, aerodynamic efficiencies, an instrument panel that floats in the cabin preventing the driver from re-focusing from the road, and air vents using Dyson's filtration systems to keep pollutants out. It looks genuinely appealing.

So why the failure? Because it would need to cost, said Dyson, at least £150,000 to cover the expensive production cost of electric vehicles, and unlike the major motor manufacturers he does not have a range of petrol and diesel cars to subsidise the cost of electric models until the cost of producing electric cars falls in time.

When Dyson started the car project, it was perhaps not foreseeable that other manufacturers would – for reason of government emissions targets and competitive reasons – sell electric cars at this time as loss-leaders, subsidised by petrol and diesel models until the production costs fall.

An expensive failure, one could argue at £500m. But not one which in my view the company should be embarrassed about. It shows what Dyson is capable of goes way beyond small domestic appliances. And really enhances the brand. And – who knows – as other motor manufacturers scramble for battery power to match Dyson's claimed 600 mile range, it's power at least might yet find a customer. As – in due course when the market changes are we are all driving battery cars – might the prospects for a Dyson car as a whole.

Business is – by definition – a risky business. Companies that make enormous margins only look clever after the event, in hindsight. Many will have been close to failure, and through luck, circumstances and anything else dodged failure by an inch and made success.

Dyson has had enough success from arguably riskier projects. Who would have thought bagless vacuum cleaners costing so much more than most competitor products would have dominated the market as they did when they first appeared.

If you wait for a 'dead cert' idea, or plan, before launching a business, or new business idea or plan, you might well be waiting forever. Of course aim for success and not failure, but the successful will have got there with a different attitude to failure – more accepting of the risk – than most people.

The talent is in spotting the moment of 'failure,' as Dyson did. It is easy once energy, time and money has been invested in a project to think it is now too big to stop, that there is just too much invested in it for there to be a moment of surrender. But if Dyson ploughed on, continuing to develop a car for launch and then selling each one at a loss would prejudice the wider Dyson business. Spotting failure and acting on it appropriately is the right approach to failure in business, rather than thinking failure is somehow avoidable.

TIP

Beware that an over-cautious approach designed to mitigate against failure may itself be the reason for failure. Planning for either success of failure can be self-fulfilling.

The path to success is giving your business the space to be creative and to invent the next globally successful best-selling product, or to come up with new ideas that customers will crave. Some – probably most of you if you are properly exploring – will fail in some respect. If you fear failure, you probably haven't got the courage required to succeed.

****

15

Hunger and entrepreneurialism

No, I'm not talking about the manager who goes for a large lunch, and early every day. We've probably all worked for or at least observed a manager who has, quite frankly, given up. Coasting. In work and probably life more generally. The look is one of blankness. The pace is pedestrian. They've checked out. They are just ticking the boxes.

Management without hunger is like a car without fuel or a human without food. It's that important. Tolerate management without hunger and your business will coast at best and fail at worst. Coasting might be fine if you're in a sector where everyone is coasting, but you will forever be at the mercy of a new entrant with hunger or a rival suddenly waking up and finding some hunger.

Business, at its heart, is about spotting commercial opportunity and delivering on it. The best businesses will employ people with the flair of entrepreneurship and furthermore those businesses will foster and grow and refine it throughout the organisation and over time.

Entrepreneurial people will look at life from a different perspective to others. They will look for elements of daily life which are imperfect in some way, and see if there is a business opportunity. When someone kept losing a can opener in the moment they needed to open a can, the invention of the can with a built-in ring-pull was born.

Entrepreneurial people will analyse words and actions for opportunity. If a massive campaign group was set up to seek to stop house builders building houses in identical, modern styles, and instead fulfil a desire for more individual and characterful properties, to the entrepreneur that might (subject to further analysis) identify a gap in the market for a housebuilder who specialises in those desires. Filling that gap might be a very successful enterprise.

A culture of entrepreneurship is desirable throughout an organisation, and not just on the part of those running the business. Opportunity and intelligence might, after all, knock at any level: the receptionist may have a discussion with a procurement manager prior to your meeting with him, in which he might happen to mention a new project he is leading, in respect of which he requires assistance. Let's imagine he doesn't know you have the capability to provide that assistance. If you do not co-incidentally have that same discussion with him, perhaps because you have a heavy agenda already, or get side-tracked on topics like family, sport or lunch once the immediate business is done, you need the receptionist to show some entrepreneurial flair by identifying the opportunity and raising it with you, so that you can (should it be a good one) explore the opportunity with the client.

Even more so at a middle and senior level is entrepreneurship important. A management team that focuses only operational or technical delivery might utterly fail to identify an idea, market or successfully take the idea to market. A team-leader with no entrepreneurial flair might limit a business by ignoring or even failing to spot opportunities.

The best outcome is when everyone acts entrepreneurially and as a team. I've had some great leads over the years spotted by junior team members with their ear to the ground, business development people have then researched the opportunity and context more fully, then I've gone in and targeted the opportunity, pulled in marketeers to help with pitch documents, and delivered the successful pitch with a team including the person who first spotted the idea. That's an entrepreneurial team effort.

At the other extreme, I've heard leaders in business development seminars complain that nobody has coached them on what targets to approach by way of business development, or dismiss it as a job for the sales teams. In my humble opinion, if a leader thinks that business development is for others it raises a question over their suitability for the title. As we have seen, even junior team members can show business development flair, and it is useful for a business for everyone to do so.

I have worked alongside workers who worry that responding promptly to a potential new business lead might lead to their in-tray being a bit too heavy, so they pause secretly hoping it might go away. Such behaviour at best leads to a zombie business, making money almost accidentally, or perhaps reluctantly, because some clients have low expectations or a high level of patience, but it will be underachieving. A good business will have recruited people with a culture of entrepreneurship, or trained them in such a thing, and will have structured the business to give them the space to always ensure it is exercised. Contrast our imagined over-burdened worker, shying away from responding to an enquiry because he's already over-worked and under-paid, with a business that has incentivised responsiveness by giving staff a bonus of 5% of the new job, if they secure it, and a free say in whether it is one for them to go on to handle or not, and spare capacity elsewhere to jump on it if the person who took the initial enquiry cannot. An even more entrepreneurial business might have structured itself so that someone senior with sales experience and ability contacts the new business lead within 24 hours to offer to visit the client and explain all about the business, the products and services offered, and to express enthusiasm for establishing a business relationship. Contrast that with the competitor who still hasn't e-mailed back after 4 days…. One can imagine where the customer will place his business. But the zombie business who doesn't get the job probably thinks it is performing. You win some jobs, you lose some, they will say. And they get enough work to pay the bills. And so they continue, in a zombie way, oblivious to the opportunity cost of failing to embed a culture of hunger and entrepreneurship across the business, in its structures and all of its people.

<u>TIP</u>

Hunger and entrepreneurialism is just for the Board and the sales manager, right? Wrong. See the difference when an organisation embeds hunger and entrepreneurialism across its entire organisation. Demand it of even your most junior hires, and see the difference.

****

16

Beware the reassurance
of the yes man…and groupthink

Some team and business leaders surround themselves with people who they think will always agree with them, and thus cement, make easier and not threaten the position of the leader. We've all seen it from time to time. A leader who surrounds himself not with a broad range of diverse talent, but instead who surrounds himself with a bunch of average people who keep the leader's favour by agreeing with his every move. The band of merry 'yes men.' This is almost always a catastrophic error of judgment.

The best decisions are usually made not by one man alone, or a group of near-identically minded people, but by a genuinely diverse mix of viewpoints and opinions. A leader surrounded by yes men could propose a terrible idea, and the yes men around him would applaud the initiative as a great one. The leader, buoyed by this approval and encouragement, would forge ahead with his bad idea with even more certainty in its success. Only for it to inevitably fail. Watching it unfold is like watching a Shakespearean tragedy.

Worse, the business will find itself at a huge competitive disadvantage to competitors who embrace a wide range of opinions in order to better inform decision-making. And, unable to see or at least vocalise the flaws in the business strategy, the yes men and their leader won't even appreciate that until, potentially, it is too late.

The problem may then be compounded by the yes men telling each other that everything is great, even when it is not. I once knew of a rather provincial business which traded from cheap out of town office space in a sector where all of its main rivals occupied city centre clean, modern office space walking distance from its clients, and where the best staff wanted to be based for that reason. For many years the board laughed at how much rivals were spending on rent close to their clients and spoke of how the cheaper remote locations meant they would always win work on price. This was a view which became heavily ingrained into the firm's senior thinking and culture, so much so that it was regularly trotted out as an obvious statement of fact and never questioned or re-visited. It was in fact a missed opportunity. The business missed out on local markets in cities they were absent from. And it missed out on the best staff, who tended to work in city centre firms for the same reason. It was a failure to understand that being local to one's customer, or at least in a place the customer does not mind visiting, and in premises the customer (and the best staff) would want to spend time, would often win an account. It was an over-simplistic conclusion that a low price alone would always win the day. But in the search for a unique selling point, a market differentiator, this became it, and the senior management trotted it out like it was their trump card. It almost became their identity. It took many years of quality potential lateral hires saying they would only be based nearer to their clients, and years of profits being squeezed, before the business eventually diversified into markets like the city of London and other commercial centres where its key target clients were based, later than all of its rivals.

It is generally the leader who is to blame for bringing about such a yes-men state of affairs. A leader who likes to be surrounded by yes men will foster such a culture by recruiting and promoting only yes men, and avoiding and driving out, actively or passively, those who do not give gushing approval to everything and thus are seen as dissenters. A sort of corporate North Korea or Zimbabwe comes from the top down.

Those genuine voices of reason trying to add some vision or perspective in the face of a bad decision will be seen as marginal – even when the view is logical and mainstream and the better one – purely because it is a lone voice amongst the yes men piping up in support of the leader's bad decision. The one wise voice becomes seen as the wrong voice among the numerous imbecilic views. Like asking a loan shark if you should borrow more when in debt. There'll be loud approval of what you are doing. But it'll be a push down the stairs not a lift up to success. It is a downward spiral.

Once this 'yes men' culture becomes embedded it holds back the entire business and is not just an influence on leadership decisions, because all people who adopt the culture of always agreeing with the leader for advancement and an easy ride always think not in terms of 'what is the right answer' but instead 'what would the leader say.' The right decision only rises to the top of the pile if it's what the leaders would say. Because the only 'yes' is what the leader would say, even if that is the wrong decision. What a waste of a potentially broad church of viewpoints, stifled by a follow-my-leader lemming culture. Of course the leader should be respected and take and be responsible for the final decision, but what leader aspires to only hear echoes of the content of his own head rather than a broad church of constructive inputs to best inform the way forward.

Democratic free states recognise the desirability of diverse Parliaments to debate and test laws and policymaking before they are made. The debate is often adversarial, and robust. Different – opposing – viewpoints are always heard. That is how ideas are truly tested. By rigorous stress testing through open debate, involving all viewpoints. Imagine a Parliament with a yes man culture where all the members just agreed with anything the Prime Minister or President suggested, without any rigorous debate bringing all viewpoints to the table first. It might work bearably for the brief term of a genius leader (if there is such a thing) but it would be hugely more vulnerable to bad decision-making. Bad ideas get traction when they are not adequately or robustly debated.

The yes man culture can arise from fear or stupidity. Beware both. Fear when the senior management can take no dissent or debate, and therefore everyone says oh yes yes yes however stupid the idea from the top, in fear of being cast aside for showing disloyalty. Stupidity when everyone is too unskilled or experienced to have any ideas or to properly analyse the ideas coming from the top, and so they agree with everything for lack of vision themselves, like 3 year olds agreeing with teacher.

In an advanced 'yes man' culture, truth and opinion can become indistinguishable from each other. Such is the nodding dog state of all meetings and communications that opinions are never challenged or tested, and opinion becomes fact.

The advocate for surrounding himself with yes men may counter that the opposite strategy – a mix of different views and open debate – only leads to division.

That is however misguided, because the best businesses are open to enabling the best decision-making by encouraging different viewpoints and open debate, but when a decision is made the entire business unites behind it, regardless of whether their individual view prevailed in the eventual vote, because they know that is part of – and the strength of – the wider team and putting the business before the individual.

The best decisions are made by a being tested by a range of viewpoints and skills, but where the crowd then unites behind a democratic decision.

An allied but subtly different problem is groupthink, where a group reach the same decision without proper debate due to a common desire not to upset the group. It's easier to say yes than be the odd one out. It feels easier to go along with the crowd than stand against it, even in a constructive way.

The business likely condemned to failure is one where everyone within the business has to some extent ceased to possess any independence of thought. At meetings everyone agrees, and to demonstrate as much they repeat each other in different words echoing the same message. There is never dissent. There is never any proper scrutiny. The group will all buy into it. There will be no departure from it. Superficially, it may sound like unity, and the avoidance of time debating things, but fundamentally no good decisions can be made unless they are first rigorously tested by a diverse panel.

And groupthink is not just something bad businessmen or employees get up to. It is a trap for us all. Joining a business ruled by groupthink will likely make you succumb to it. Imagine you are in a meeting where every other 29 participants all agree and waste an hour making the same point in various ways to demonstrate as much. Even if you are sitting there observing the opinions as demonstrable nonsense, you'll be hard pushed to break free and be the one dissenting voice in the room. In such a business, dissent (because it is unheard of) will shock, alienate, and probably kibosh any career advancement whatsoever. Before long, you'll find your lips mouthing the words *"well there is something in that,"* even when your brain is decisively convinced there is precisely nothing in that.

Before long, however, if you spend too much time with your head in groupthink, you will fall prey to it and go native, precisely because of the relative or complete absence of challenging voices. There is always a narrative in support of any particular view. To Putin's Russia, NATO somehow caused Russia to invade Ukraine. It is a view repeated so often, and as persuasively as it can be, that many Russians believe it. It is obvious nonsense. Russia unilaterally invaded a non-NATO country entirely of its own initiative. But repeated widely, with few or no dissenting voices, even an obvious idiotic narrative becomes the accepted one within a group. The Nazis in Germany were propaganda masters of leading groupthink: shut out dissenting or even challenging voices, repeat a message often enough and with sufficient force, and before you know it, the view is the only one in the room and accepted widely even if demonstrably false.

Groupthink can be at its most dangerous when it does not result in early failure. If it causes the collapse of a business, or venture, it is exposed. If we observe such a failure properly, it is the best advertisement against groupthink: 'there's a business that was taken down by groupthink.' A failure puts a brutal stop to the nonsense and lessons can be learned. However, if groupthink is not so bad as to result in failure, but simply surviving mediocrity, it can be even worse. The survival of the groupthink business can be seen by the group as vindication of the groupthink: 'how sensible we were to become a bunch of one-tone idiots lazily plodding on never testing or thinking outside the box; it has led to our survival while others have gone under, so we must continue! More groupthink!' Oh dear. Groupthink even when it occurs within a surviving business will result in under-performance. Mediocrity, rather than brilliance, or at least achieving your full potential. Do not think your survival vindicates groupthink. Realise that groupthink is leading you to little better than survival. To realise your full potential, and be brilliant rather than merely surviving, will require you to ditch the groupthink. And groupthink within a business leads to a lingering vulnerability. You might survive, if not thrive, until a competitor comes along without the disease of groupthink: then your days are numbered. The groupthink business will go under, but (groupthinking to the last) they'll tell themselves something external outside of their control was the wicked cause of the end. Better to wake up earlier.

TIP

A business with a yes man culture will only be as good as the mind of its decision-makers. Likewise a business overcome by groupthink. Ideas will never be subject to proper scrutiny, just the echo chamber of adoration from the yes men. Distinguish the very healthy trait of diverse debate from disunity. Embrace a culture of debate and see how it elevates the success of your decision-making.

****

17

A business run by the accountants

Many accountants are lovely people, and they undoubtedly form a key role in business. But danger can lurk when the accountants take charge rather than being merely advisors whose insight informs wider decision-making.

Accountants tend to view 'figures as figures' on spreadsheets, and it is down to the commercial management to add a layer of real-world analysis. One way in which this often manifests itself is a focus on cost, rather than value. An accountant might suggest that axing a sales team could save combined salaries of £500,000 a year. That might sound great, if the business is targeting that sort of funding for a new project or new equipment, or if the business has taken a downturn and savings need to be made. But what if the team of salesmen were what really kept the sales coming in. What if they didn't just sign terms and conditions when a new account was opened, but really stayed close to the customers and nurtured them. What if they were the real reason the customers kept returning. What if those salesmen *were* essentially the business. A saving of £500,000 in saved salaries could end up costing the business £50 million in customer revenue.

A spreadsheet that dictates any investment must have a, say, 50%+ return might decline to hire a key man just because he is demanding a salary £25k higher than the default accounting formula for that key return on investment calculation. But what if that hire was the next Richard Branson, Bill Gates or James Dyson. You wouldn't want to miss out over £25k annually. The spreadsheet wouldn't hire. The entrepreneur would.

An accountant once reviewed a business and advised its owners that it was making a terrible mistake by paying invoices on the day they were received. They should be paid no earlier than day 30 – the due date – thought the accountant. That way the business could earn interest on its cash for those extra 30 days. The business owner pointed out that by paying on time he was always front of the queue with all of his suppliers, they would be more responsive thanks to his prompt payment, and he could secure special pricing and terms that nobody else could. Those advantages were significantly greater even in simple financial terms than any modest amount of interest that could be earned. In the narrow context of a spreadsheet, the accountant had come up with a good idea. But the wider business context revealed it was a terrible idea. Use data to inform decision-making, but use much more than just data too.

Large house building firms sometimes lapse into management by spreadsheet. A manager might specify smaller joists to save £50 per house, at a saving across 500,000 houses of £25 million. He might take a £125k bonus for himself for finding a way to save money and increase margin. But now the houses are built with joists right on the minimum specification. Floors are saggy and move. Rather than feeling solid. Buyers perceive the houses as cheaply made. Online reviews and word of mouth becomes negative. Everyone starts avoiding the builder that builds 'houses of straw.' House sales fall annually, causing revenue to drop by more than the 'saving' originally achieved. Spending increases on marketing and 'quality control' to try to rescue a damaged reputation. The man who 'saved' money has moved away. His slashing of spending now looks less like a margin raiser and more like a quality control and reputation destroyer.

Accountants might also be cautious about the sort of spending sometimes necessary to break through into real success. Let's say a £20 million production facility is needed to tender for a lucrative £200 million a year contract. On a spreadsheet, that might look like a heavy capital investment for an uncertain return. But the business owner might know his market. He might know his rivals have ageing plants, incapable of matching the quality and productivity of a new plant. He might know the potential supplier very well, having courted its owners for 10 years. He might know they are ready for a change. And that the investment, and the trust built up over the time a relationship has been nurtured, would give them the perfect reason to make that change. The full story makes it likely you would make a very different decision about whether to spend the money than from just the bare numbers on a page. Look at the numbers, have a mastery of them even, but realise that successful business is about a much wider context.

Management by spreadsheet can lead to musical chairs. In other words, looking only at the numbers on a page, one can be tempted to shuffle them around between columns, to hail the change as a success, when in reality it is of marginal if any impact at all. An example is the insurance industry, which at times has laid off its internal talent to reduce payroll, only to in other times beef up internal recruitment to avoid external costs. Redundancies can be dressed up as a significant cost saving, and boost to profits. But so can axing higher outsourcing costs and in-housing that cost by way of extra recruitment instead. One could flip the policy every few years to claim a 'success,' but all that would do in reality would just add cost associated with redundancies, outsourcing and hiring.

Accounting policies can also lead to misleading results. For example, accountants will often 'write off' the value of an invoice if it is older than say 6 months. Because after such a time it becomes at risk of never being paid, and a 'bad debt.' If the invoice is then paid in month seven, it might be seen as '100% pure profit' because it was something that had already been written off. But the write off changed nothing, and it is not '100% pure profit.' Indeed, the same cost of sales went into the sale, regardless of whether payment is made by the customer in month 5 or month 7. To describe the income as 'pure profit' would be misleading, because the invoice of say £10,000 cannot in reality be added in its totality to the profit bottom line, because that implies that there were no costs involved in the sale. If it cost £5,000 to buy the goods which were sold for £10,000, then the profit is £5,000 whether payment is made in month 5 or month 7. To describe it as 'pure profit' just because it is paid after a write-off is misleading because it ignores the £5,000 cost, and thus overstates the profit by £5,000. Let's say there were 100 of these invoices, paid late, every year. The accounting policy would record it as £500k pure profit, when we know given the purchasing cost it is only £250k (gross) profit. The remainder would be lurking somewhere under bad debt provision.

Accounting policies have their place, but always ultimately see and be grounded in the inescapable factual reality.

TIP

Numbers can seem compelling, but beware their allure without the fuller context. Have a mastery of the numbers, but don't run your business entirely by spreadsheet.

****

18

Micromanagement

In order for a business to thrive, you must fill it with talented people and give them what they need to perform and deliver.

It is tempting, especially for new promotees to a management role, to think that because the buck stops with them, and because junior people cannot be completely trusted to perform, it is necessary to micro-manage everything that those they are responsible do.

At its worst, the micro-manager will cling onto everything. He is rushing around without enough hours in the day, while his team sits relatively idle. If challenged, he will be very defensive: *"you can't trust these kids with a task like this. If I do it myself, it's right first time."* Very often that is untrue because if the manager did his job properly and recruited suitable people to work under him, properly supported, then they would be capable.

Even where this is a whisker of truth in such a statement – where the team leader is more experienced and more capable than his team – the job at hand may nevertheless be dealt with better across the team. Even if the manager's input is required, in most cases it may be a better balance for the team to handle but with the manager dipping in to add extra value where required: the CEO of Asda, for example, might express a view on the layout of the entrance lobby of each store, but he would probably by better served allowing store managers to handle the physical layout implementation on a store by store level, as opposed to being out of action for weeks micro-managing every element of that himself. A CEO can probably add more value by having a focus elsewhere.

Alternatively, the micro-manager may let go but insufficiently, wrongly thinking he needs control of every element of the business, small as well as large, even if he allows others to work under his instruction. I knew of a CEO who paid very little interest at all to how the key people in the business cared for clients and delivered for them (the key aspects of a service business one may think), but demanded that he be consulted for all sorts of internal details such as writing off any recorded time over £500 in value, raising a client bill, or for pre-approving expense like client lunches. The poor man probably never had time for any big picture strategic thinking, so floored was he with day to day admin. The more effective manager might appoint a finance manager to deal with all of that, and give key people in the business budgets they might require. The CEO would then be set free to *do his job*, ie, come up with new ideas, manage relationships, focus on continuous improvement, etc.

The micromanager might be innocently committing his crime, perhaps because he doesn't know what his job is. The first-time just-promoted leaders might stay mired in admin and looking over the shoulder of employees *because he thinks that is management.* He might need a nudge to say would you be better off getting the right people and empowering them to do those things, to free you up to do leadership...? Like business planning, inspiring, holding together a business-wide ethos, mentoring, etc.

Micromanaging can be possible for a small business or sole trader, but if you are bigger than that or have ambition to be, you will have to learn to move away from the habit. It will hold you back. Realise who you need in what role, and then set them free to make it happen. Keep a bigger picture view from the centre. The same is true even if you aren't in overall charge. A team manager must learn to delegate and focus just as much as a CEO. If you supervise the entire team's entire work, direct their every move, and give them no real freedom or authority, either because you've not recruited the right people for the right roles, or just for control, you'll be doing no more than what your team should be doing, and you'll not be doing what you should be doing – focusing on improvements, monitoring performance, having the space to analyse and come up with new ideas, manage relationships, etc.

When a leader micromanages everything he is limiting the potential of his business that day to the number of decisions he can make in a day. The leaders who appoints, say, six key managers for each part of his business – each with the necessary ability and empowered to act and make decisions – can potentially thereby make the business six times greater. If everything is done by you then the potential of the business is limited by your time and energy. Get the right team assembled, and the potential multiplies.

Micromanagement can be a distraction from real management. Imagine two cafes. One gets all the key business ingredients right – a seasonal local top quality menu, great chefs, a wide range of fabulous drinks, etc. The second café serves over-priced rubbish. The former is doing £1 million a year. The latter is losing money every month. The first café owner has focused on the business essentials – the right product, service, venue, and so on. And he's left those in charge of each area to then get on with it. The second café owner is running around asking his staff why the customers are not coming in, and why revenue is not higher. He is having daily crisis meetings with the team. He's trying to negotiate 10% off with suppliers. And is offering 10% off coupon days to try – unsuccessfully – to get customers in. He's watching every staff member like a hawk trying to work out where the business is going 'wrong.' The truth is, what is wrong is his own lack of a successful business model. He needs to stop desperately and fruitlessly tweaking and micromanaging, and instead step back and deliver the successful business model, which will involve him intervening less in the minutiae and focusing more on the big picture.

TIP

Effective leaders at all levels do not micromanage the day to day minutiae of what the rest of the team is doing. They hire the right people and set them free. And then they get on with genuine leadership. Learn to know the difference.

****

19

Emotional intelligence

Conventional wisdom tells us that we should leave our emotions at home when we enter the workplace. Work is something separate to emotions, which belong instead at home and in our private lives. The truth is, however, more likely that we do take our emotions into the workplace, and always will, however hard we might try not to.

A lot of businesses are dysfunctional because they know nothing about – and lack – emotional intelligence, namely being aware of your emotions and developing an ability to control them for the good of the desired outcome, in the way you might control the words you use of physical behaviour. Still less do they train and foster emotional intelligence across the organisation.

The main reason may be ignorance. What do we really mean by emotional intelligence? Some examples might help.

Think of a situation in a working environment when you were last angry. Did you realise you were angry? When? In the moment, or later, and how later? Did you realise why you were angry? If you had no or incomplete self-awareness of the emotion and its reasons, looking back now did that cause a situation to escalate, or cause you to not get the best out of the moment? Were you angry and your facial expression, body language, words and actions showed that? You might have shouted and stormed off leaving others worried and focusing on that rather than progress. Or were you able to recognise anger and its reasons and then – after that moment of self-awareness, consider how best to deal with that in the moment. For example if a colleague had not done their contribution to a joint document on time, would you shout and walk away and do it yourself, or would you be able to say 'I'm a little angry that the rest of the group have all done their individual contributions but you haven't – can you help us understand why and can we discuss how to remedy the gap we are left with?' You can see how the latter might be better in terms of sorting the issue out in the moment. The failing team member might be able to offer a good explanation – a domestic emergency, and others might then offer to pull together to cover. Rather than anger causing the whole group to struggle to focus, and causing the outcome to be in jeopardy.

Can you stay positive even in a negative moment, or does a negative moment de-rail you easily and for the rest of the day? In the example above it would be easy to think, 'we can't even pull together and draft a document as a team – this team and this project is a failure.' But one can see how it might be better – for the team and the project – to instead think, 'it's only one contribution to the whole, and the rest of the team can complete the missing ingredient this afternoon, and we can still be on time.'

Can you control your emotions in a crisis? If you were the team member without their contribution to the group project completed, because of a domestic crisis, would the combination of domestic stress, work pressure, fear of failure and its consequences, and guilt of having let the wider team down de-rail you, or even in the heat of the moment could you control your emotions and explain and move forwards, more in the spirit of an objective onlooker, rather than the person in the eye of the storm?

Can you empathise with others? Does the project leader merely think 'this one team member is a disgrace – he's let the team and the project down'? Does the team member without their contribution done merely think 'nobody cares about me I'm so on my own? Or instead could they, by trying to see the situation through the eyes of others in the group – and trying to understand everyone else's words and actions accordingly – stay more united and stay better able to react positively to the situation?

What about change? Imagine that you've been pondering the project topic for weeks, and you've brainstormed, discussed and drafted. The project leader announces that the client has changed the topic at the last minute. And the deadline is still tonight! Do you become paralysed by disappointment, panic, anger, and pressure? Or do you think calmly, not about what has gone before and the sudden change, but instead about what needs to be done: 'the brief has changed, we all need to deliver a lot in a short timescale, let's talk about how we ace this brief on time.' Imagine being given a changed brief and short deadline. You could spend the next 2 hours saying how it can't be done, how outrageous a late change is, or you could spend that 2 hours *getting it done* instead. The emotionally aware employee will quickly recognise the potentially paralysing emotions of panic, pressure and so on, realise that those emotions will prevent the job getting done rather than help it, control those emotions to prevent them paralysing performance, and quietly get on with getting the job done.

And it is not only negative emotions that it helps to be aware of and control. Imagine winning a new customer. You feel rightly pleased and celebratory. But if the customer is expecting an acknowledgment and a first piece of work done this afternoon, unconsciously and immediately – in a mood of tidal-wave celebration – clocking off the whole team as soon as the 'win' comes in and going drinking for the rest of the afternoon and evening might harm the recent win. Better to think 'joy – we must celebrate – but after we call the client and get this first quick job done,' and announce timetable to the team. The win would thereby be cemented and the later celebration all the more deserved.

Better decisions are made when emotionally aware, as well as interactions with others. When looking at several options and choosing between them, to what extent are emotions colouring your judgment? A CEO might be mulling an offer from another company to buy the business. He owns 20% of the business in shares. He could be £10m richer this year if the sale takes place. Imagine the feeling of joy. It might compel him to say deal done, or recommend it to the wider Board. But what if the price offered is 33% below market value? Putting his own personal emotions – joy of personal gain and financial freedom – aside, would the right thing to do be to recommend rejection of the offer?

In the same way as recognising your own emotions can help, then being able to recognise them in others can also help. If you see a colleague in an explosive rage, for example, spotting anger and realising its likely negative effect, you might suggest a short break to let the anger subside before the meeting resumes.

TIP

Being emotionally intelligent is not, as its bad press sometimes (out of ignorance) suggests, being soft or lacking the hard edge to be successful in business. On the contrary, the emotionally intelligent business can steal a massive advantage on its competitors will surprisingly little investment cost.

****

20

Responsiveness

One of my frequent pieces of advice to junior lawyers is, if you respond to clients quickly then you are instantly in the top 10% or so of lawyers regardless of anything else, because most lawyers do not respond quickly. They take their time. If you e-mail or call in and leave a message, it might take a couple of days for the firm internally to find the right person to respond, then another day for them to find time to contact you. Contrast that with a firm that telephones you within an hour of your initial enquiry, offers you a meeting the next day, and before the other firm has even made initial contact with you, the quicker firm has signed you up and is cracking on with the job. Don't lose even opportunities by just being too slow.

I've known bad businesses confuse issues in this regard. They might say for example 'customers need to understand we are busy and can't just drop everything for them at any time of day.' That is not a reason not to be responsive. How about responding immediately (ie, anyone in the business send the response) to say something like, 'thanks for the message, we want to discuss, we are out on site and imagine coming back to you further this evening.' Most customers will be impressed enough by that. It's about having the courtesy to respond and setting a timetable for what happens next. To suggest it is about the customer having to know you are too busy to respond immediately is to miss the point, and to put ego before good business.

Other bad business attitude is to think 'we don't just want to respond to any old dross and end up weighed down by bad jobs.' Again, this is illogical. You don't necessarily have to take on a job just because you respond to it. The point is about exploring opportunity. If you're too slow to respond and miss out, how will you know if it was a £10k job or a £10 million job...? Responding promptly and courtesy will ensure that you keep the door of opportunity open, and probably while everyone else is being slow give yourself first pick of every job.

I've also heard 'make them wait so they know how important we are.' Oh dear. Let's hope they are still waiting by the time you do reply, so that you get the chance to demonstrate 'how important you are.' A humble responsiveness beats ego getting in the way of customer service and relationships.

Responsiveness is also about reputation. Even if you don't necessary work with a customer this time around, for whatever reason, being responsive might mean you do work together in the future, or that you bag a recommendation. Consider a builder who quotes you £20k above the price you go for instead on a job, but who was first to respond and whose communication was impeccable. The alternative builder you went with on the first job turned out to be slow to respond to everything during the job and did a reasonable but not superb job. Next time around you might well consider the more responsive builder! And you might say if asked, even before you've even used him, that the builder who impressed you with his communications 'might be first choice if you want someone who's quick to respond.' Imagine the value in being top of people's minds the next time around, and in getting free promotions. All as the reward for being responsive. Responsiveness can be as valuable as a very expensive marketing or PR budget, yet cost you nothing.

A lack of responsiveness can imply – rightly or wrongly – that you don't have the resource or simply cannot be bothered to respond promptly. Neither create a good impression in the minds of people you might want to do business with. Imagine a customer thinking 'they're struggling to cope: it takes anyone there a week to respond' when actually the slowness is not because of a lack of resource but just the wrong approach. It is a short step from an assumption of a lack of resource to a lack of ability. If you aren't responding promptly, is it because you don't know how to...! Don't let a valued customer's wrong assumptions creep in by simply failing to respond promptly.

Responsiveness can also add value. In the example of the builders above, first time around you thought the man who was £20k more was 'too expensive.' Second time around, after suffering the relative torture of someone who was slow to deal with. Astute customers will realise that time is money, and that there is enormous value in someone who can act quickly. If you wait a day for a response to everything, as opposed to an hour, think of the extra time – and cost – that adds to a job. As a result the responsive supplier can expect to be able to charge more, and make a greater margin. Without adding anything to the cost side of the balance sheet.

And if you think you are doing ok without being a rapid responder, consider that the reverse is also true: the slow responder is at risk of having his reputation and margin eroded by his own tardiness. Imagine hearing a review along the lines of 'oh gosh you'll still be waiting at Christmas to hear back from them!' or 'bearable if they are standing in front of you but try getting a response when they are not...!' Ouch. Still think you are doing ok? And consider the impact on the number of jobs you get, and what you are able to charge, of all that.

Responsiveness is not just about new work opportunities. It is a key part of developing existing customer and supplier relationships. To quote an adage, 'you're only ever as good as your most recent job.' It's no good being quick to respond to a new client initially, only to then lapse into laziness. That just looks like a cynical snare to net new customers and then treat them less well once they are through the door. Which is possibly even worse than just being true to yourself and slow from the start. Being prompt to respond will rightly earn you a loyal following. If you need a quick response you probably know which suppliers to go to. And they'll have earned that sort of reputation and loyalty.

TIP

Don't wrongly think being responsive shows weakness or is trivial.
Earn a reputation for being prompt to respond and reap the rewards.

****

21

Talking to the right people

A point which is perhaps obvious once you consider it but which is often overlooked by many is the importance of getting to the right person. The perfect content, perfectly delivered, is still wasted if you are talking to the wrong person. The right audience can be even more important than the right content.

In the early days in my own profession, law, I might have approached a legal person within an organisation, assuming that is where the synergy and authority might lie to involve external lawyers. Often however in-house lawyers are a busy and overworked bunch, and might be reluctant to take a new idea or project to the business in fear of it simply meaning yet more to add to their own workload. Their own targets tend to motivate them to get through a legal postbag, and they wouldn't get the credit for a new idea or project anyway. That is no criticism of the in-house lawyers: it just isn't their job. Procurement might be another obvious target, since they have direct responsibility for approving suppliers, but would they necessarily see the need for it, or is their role to manage a process when asked to do so internally? Does it properly need someone else to see the need, and to then involve procurement to scrutinise the appointment?

If I saw a way legal services could be delivered in a way to save that business money or deliver better results for that business, I might go to the person with an interest in and responsibility for the bottom line, ie maximising results and keeping cost as low as possible, who might be more interested in the initial idea than legal or procurement, and who would then involve those other teams once the pitch was successful, and to implement it.

Equally if someone approached me with the perfect pitch for a new cleaning service, even if I liked the sound of it and thought it would transform the business, it isn't something within my day to day responsibilities, I am busy enough already, and they'd have probably been better off pitching to the facilities manager with a more direct interest in, and responsibility for, such things.

Sometimes this is the reason for a business pitching to investors like on BBC Dragons' Den. The value in the investor might be the contacts in their address book just as much as any cash investment. Because an astute entrepreneur knows that the right contacts are the key to the door. A superb product might have been blanked by cold calls or e-mails to the wrong contacts. It might be a £ multi million deal if the right contacts speak directly.

I have lost track of the organisations I didn't get into on the first attempt, but later have a great experience or relationship with. It can be all about the right person at the right time.

It isn't about excluding anyone, or stepping on toes, or going behind people's backs, as some people perhaps sometimes fear, but about getting to the right person who will listen because he or she is interested, and has the ability to say yes and make it happen, then with the support of all those wider teams who you can then meet and develop relationships with too.

You might well devise a series of subtly different messages to appeal to all aspects of the business you are talking to. It would be the same product or service, but the message tailored for each different audience. To a finance director, one might focus on the impact on the numbers. To the branding people, one might go large on branding synergy! To the buyers, how fabulous your product or service is! Targeting a message to the audience is often half the success.

TIP

A perfect pitch to the wrong ears is a flower blooming unseen on the desert floor. Get to the right person for your message. If there are various messages, deliver them to the right ears across the business or organisation.

****

22

Relationships not transactions

One of the biggest lessons I have learned in business is to strive for relationships over individual transactions. Too many people, motivated by the greed of this month's revenue figures, put a fat bill ahead of any relationship. So to hit their own target and get their bonus they will bill customers or client figures in the knowledge the client or customer will be shocked, and might not even return. Perhaps the costs estimate was £25k, but the bill is going to be £35k. Put it through, and hope for the best. It'll nail this month's billing target. But what if it kills a relationship.

Successful relationships give you years – perhaps tens of years – of a customer relationship. That obviously gives you a long relationship that produces revenue. It makes business easier to predict than if you are instead simply reliant on a series of individual transactions, perhaps from customers who just buy once and do not return.

A relationship requires more than just transactions to establish itself, but the pay back is greater than the extra investment. So a car seller might stay in touch every couple of months with new model news, they might offer 10% off servicing, and they might hand hold you through exchange time ahead of you approaching them for a sale. The greedy seller might think why 'throw away' all that added value with no added charge. But the seller who appreciates the importance of relationships knows that such investment is worth it for a customer who returns another 20 times rather than being a customer only for a single transaction, then off to another seller, perhaps one who knows the importance of relationships over transactions.

And if a relationship doesn't last forever, well not all of them do. But overall relationships will produce more than the absence of them. If you aren't maintaining relationships, ask rather than seeing that as proof they are a waste of investment whether you are doing it as well as your best competitors. If a relationship moves elsewhere, it might be because someone else is doing it better.

With one off relationships, there is a lot of work in every transaction. In a longer-term relationship, the ground work is largely done once and then a repetition of that in every transaction is saved. For example, there might be a lot of understanding, data gathering and rapport building at the start of dealings with a new customer. That groundwork is largely done if they return for a second sale, so you save time repeating all that groundwork. The second sale is a more efficient one. If repeat sales are 10% more efficient, you could offer a 5% discount and still be 5% better off.

Relationships, if nurtured, become easier over time. If a relationship is treated well, trust and understanding embeds itself, and that makes delivering and communicating much easier. With further savings in time down the line. For example, if I trust a supplier I might be more forgiving of a small mistake than I would be with a new supplier. If that maintains a relationship that lasts for another 20 years imagine the value of that.

Parties with an existing relationship are also more likely to be more loyal. Why go to a new supplier if you have a long and positive relationship with an existing one?

A business more interested in maximising revenue from one-off transactions by a failure to see the benefit of doing the things that build relationships (discounting, complimentary added value, and so on) might do better on a single transaction viewed in isolation, and assessed only by sale price, but the greedy business not interested in relationships might before too long find its customers tied into relationships with other suppliers who are more interested in relationships.

You might think relationships must only be for complex or high value markets. How for example can a volume business develop relationships with customers? A supermarket chain, for example. How can you sell tinned baked beans to consumers and foster a relationship? Well, when a supermarket delivered my 100th order, it included a free hamper to say thank you. And it texts with the driver's name, always from the local supermarket, so you can feel like you 'know' the small pool of drivers. In truth, a relationship, of some kind at least, is possible in any market.

TIP

Think about relationships with your customers as long-term. If you treat them in an entirely short-term way, they might not be with you beyond that.

****

23

The over-monitoring and measurement trap

There is an increasing trend towards businesses hiring huge numbers of people who are not engaged in the business' main *raison d'etre* but instead in the side business of monitoring and measuring everything. So for example a medical clinic which employs 25 doctors and surgeons might also hire 25 administrators or 'middle managers' to monitor and measure everything. Let's call them the monitors.

The rise of the monitors is motivated by the superficial idea that by endlessly monitoring and measuring one can safeguard success. So a monitor might for example decide or be charged with monitoring that doctors see at least ten patients a day, to ensure the business makes at least ten fees per doctor per day.

The monitors might say that such monitoring is generating a certain revenue for the business. But the truth may be that the doctors might generate that revenue themselves. There is a risk that we mis-attribute outcomes to the monitors, rather than the actual workers engaged in the real activity the business is engaged in, so that we might say Bob Smith, the Head of Output Management, monitors all doctor activity to protect a minimum revenue of £50 million annually. Without a pause to consider that carefully, it can make it sound as if Bob is contributing very much indeed. He is protecting a large revenue figure. We must pay him well. And give him a bonus. And we should probably build a team around him. But is Bob actually contributing anything at all? Or would the 25 doctors produce the same or very similar outcomes even without Bob in the business. If so, Bob (and his team) while sounding very productive may just be a cost drag on the business while having no real positive impact on revenue at all.

Once such monitors become (mis) credited with the outcomes of the workers they may start to over-reach an initial brief of monitoring and start over-measuring, so that for example the doctors might be charged with billing 8 hour days instead of 7 hour days. If the doctors did that, Bob and his team might take the credit for it. Our productivity push has generated a 15% surge in profits, they might claim. Again, as if the doctors for themselves could not have worked that out.

It can all feel like a great takeover. The monitors in charge. The people engaged in the real activity of the business subservient. The tail wagging the dog. That can have a costly adverse impact on morale, productivity and success. Imagine being a doctor (or whatever) stripped of your daily focus on client care, good judgement and business, and instead reporting to a monitor who questions your every move. When it happens, the monitors will point to their monitoring and blame the doctors, or whoever. But it might be the great depressing cloud of the great takeover which is in truth to blame. If some of the doctors only manage 7.5 billable hours instead of 8 then they might find themselves denied a payrise while the middle managers take big bonuses for their monitoring and claiming the output of the doctors for themselves.

Who is to say that measurement is good or harmful? In recruitment, for example, employees can be targeted on number of outgoing emails and calls. This might encourage people being called about jobs ill-suited to them, or ill-suited CVs being submitted for jobs. That might earn the recruitment company a very bad reputation among both candidates and businesses, which in turn might hit their performance very badly. The Bobs of the world, the monitors, might be claiming big bonuses for doubling the number of outgoing calls and emails, assuming that to be a good thing, whereas in fact it is the opposite. Might it be better to focus on hiring the very best recruiters or doctors (or whatever) and setting them free to perform brilliantly. Might that produce very much better results than over-monitoring.

Do the monitors know what to monitor and optimise? In professional services, for example, the middle managers might in the name of cost cutting have axed a lot of people doing useful work, such as personal assistants, and claiming the credit for such savings at the same time as ironically consuming such savings by their own salaries. The bigger irony being that the monitors don't free up the professional workers to do only billable tasks, in the way the PAs might have done, and instead burden the professionals with endless monitoring. If the professionals are then wasting 2 hours of their day with non-chargeable administration, instead of billing £x per hour on the real activity of the business, has sacking the PAs resulted in a net negative? Two steps backwards, dressed up as a step forwards.

A surrender to monitors running the business can give an impression of success when the opposite is the case. If a retail chain goes out of business, for example, for a failure to keep up with trends, or perhaps a failure to match the quality of competition on the high street, it might come as a big surprise to the manager who had been monitoring the speed with which staff stacked shelves, or the number of transactions processed by checkout staff in an hour. Have internal monitoring if you must, or perhaps if it is helpful, but do not mistake that for real leadership, which commands a mastery of observation of the market and ensures the business is performing well within it. The best businesses focus primarily on brilliance, of the product or service they provide, and their relationship with their customers, and not on middle management daily monitoring.

And where does it end? If you are going to have a monitor for everything you would certainly end up bankrupt. If you monitor productivity and speed, as a counter to that do you need another team managing quality? If you measure number of calls made in a day, do you need another team to monitor the usefulness of those call? And so on. You would end up with ten times the number of middle managers monitoring everything than actual employees doing the real work of the business.

More fundamentally, who is going to monitor the monitors? They often seem curiously free of the sort of scrutiny they themselves exert on the productive staff in the business. Which does not help in the inexorable rise of the trend in the shift of power towards the monitors, and can lead to justified feelings of unfairness.

It came become an endless cycle into a black hole of nothingness. If the monitors are allowed to claim the credit for the productivity actually generated by the doctors, recruiters, or other productive workers, there may be an inevitable temptation to re-invest any on-paper 'savings' into yet more monitors!

And perhaps most of all, where is the creativity in monitoring and measuring? Some of my very best work in business has been done when I have a spare hour and a blank sheet of paper to brainstorm and come up with ideas. Any monitor would view such time as a total waste. They would have had me emptying 10 waste paper bins instead to satisfy a housekeeping efficiency spreadsheet. But what if the opportunity cost of some creative time is ideas worth £ millions. Would emptying bins, or whatever 'productive' activity the monitors would have us do instead, achieve that?

TIP

Stay focused on the people doing the useful work, and do not allow a business to be taken over by the bureaucrats obsessed by monitoring and measurement for its own sake and / or just for their own sake. When a business allows the over monitoring and measurement trap to squeeze out good judgement and creativity, it becomes a zombie business.

****

24

Communicate your value

In legal services, conveyancing teams often complain about low fixed fees and high caseloads. If a conveyancer has an annual billing target of £200,000, and the average fixed fee conveyance brings in £1,000, she needs to do over 16 completions a month on average to hit that target. It can lead to busy days.

Contrast the way much of the conveyancing market has gone, to low fixed fees, with the way other legal services operate. I have known people pay say £50k in legal fees to litigate a dispute worth say £100k to them. Yet they complain at a conveyancing fee of say £4k when buying a house for £1 million. Purely in investment-to-value-at-stake terms, it looks like it would make sense spending more to protect the £1 million asset purchase than on a dispute worth only 10% of that amount.

It may be that the conveyancers have failed to communicate their value. They have allowed the market to think conveyancing is just a bit of form filling and mindless process. So not worth much in terms of a fee.

Yet the litigators have comparatively communicated their value better. A knowledge of law, strategy, tactics and a mastery of evidence and language is (once communicated in that way) seen as being worth more.

Those who have come unstuck and have experienced 'cheap' conveyancing factories fail to spot and advise on key restrictions on title or other such hazards will, on the other side of such disaster, suddenly appreciate the value in a proper amount of time and skill being devoted to the task.

Not all conveyancers charge low fees. The top end of the market might charge more like £8k or so. They are communicating their value better than the low end and reaping the rewards. Of course, a quality pitch will require quality people and processes. But if you are doing say 800 completions a year in a conveyancing team, at £1k per transaction that is £800k; at £8k per transaction that is £6.4 million. The latter team can afford to pay people properly, give them the proper amount of time, invest in proper processes, and still be more profitable.

I am not against price competition and indeed it is part of any successful business. But you will maximise sales and find a higher price point in any given market by mastering the skill of communicating value.

An Apple MacBook Air sells from around £1,000.00. An Asus Chromebook sells for around £150.00. Now the MacBook may be technically superior in some ways, but they are both lightweight small laptops. A very price sensitive customer, one looking for the cheapest price regardless of other factors, might buy the Asus. Apple has found a way to communicate extra value in its product. I have not seen the internal management accounts, but I suspect there is more of a profit margin in the Apple product. Apple wins by communicating its value in useability, integrated hardware and software, design, battery life, etc.

In the 1990s, the phrase 'Mondeo man' was coined to describe the new affluent middle classes. But ten years later Mondeo sales had tanked and Mondeo man was driving a BMW 3 Series or Mercedes C Class. BMW and Mercedes had better sold the value of their medium sized saloon cars, despite them costing more, with 'premium materials,' technology, styling and performance etc. BMW and Mercedes won by better communicating the value of their products.

If you cannot communicate your value effectively, the likely consequence will be to solely compete on price instead. And at its worst, because someone else will always be willing to be cheaper (someone even worse at communicating their value and even more aggressive about lowering price), that can be a downward spiral into insolvency.

> ## TIP
>
> Whatever your price point, consider how best to communicate your value. Otherwise you might be left wondering why nobody sees your value, leaving you to under-achieve on sales and / or be left racing to the bottom on price.

****

25

Action! 'Think forward' to avoid inertia

Doing nothing is a powerful human instinct. It can be uncomfortable to have to think about doing something. For example, pursuing a desired customer, or challenging a supplier on lead times, potentially involves a lot of thinking and activity. You might you tell yourself in the present moment get away with doing nothing, hoping those issues do not have a future negative impact.

It might be more comfortable to do nothing because doing something involves a lot more. It's the same human impulse as whether to go for a job round the block. It might be tempting to stay on the sofa and do nothing. And if that impulse can kick in to prevent something as easy as a jog round the block, imagine how that impulse can apply to numerous business scenarios, which are invariably more complex than a jog around the block.

However, generally doing nothing is more painful in the long run. For example, not pursuing a desired customer might eventually lead to a lack of customers and insolvency. Or not challenging a supplier on lead times might cripple your competitiveness and eventually lead to the same catastrophic outcome.

The solution to the peril of inertia in the moment can be to think not of the present moment but instead to 'think forward' to the day when today's inertia might have an impact. The question is thus re-framed not as 'can I be bothered to chase this new customer today' to 'do I want to do this or do I want the business to fail?' Similarly, challenging a supplier on lead times becomes a question not in the present moment of shall I let sleeping dogs lie for today but instead thinking forwards do I want this discussion now to prevent my competitiveness being crippled and suffering all the bad consequences of that in the future.

If that still isn't a sufficient motivator, one can focus in a greater amount of detail. Imagine the moment of the business finding it doesn't have enough customers to pay its costs base. Imagine being in that moment. Perhaps at a defined point in the future. Let's say one year from now. You are looking at the financials and seeing more going out than coming in every day. And let's say winning a new customer takes realistically at least six months. And the cash in the bank isn't going to keep going for that long. Imagine that world of pain. Or imagine the supply chain issues causing one customer after another to walk away to a competitor, with an even quicker race to financial failure. Imagine being there in the moment. And you are then hopefully better able to balance the choice of doing nothing today versus suffering all that pain the future.

This isn't to promote over-exaggeration and to see hyperactivity as the only solution to every imagined doom. You probably don't reasonably (at least most of the time) need to have a private investigator see whether your competitors are planning to stitch you up and close you down. That is (probably, without more) pure paranoia. But if you have good instincts and a good sense for things in business, then when you identify issues doing something to fix them today is almost always better than the bigger pain tomorrow. Overall, the discomfort of acting every day to steer things in a better direction is nothing compared to the discomfort of letting everything slide for an 'easy' life today but at the risk of much worse discomfort tomorrow. Moreover, the mild discomfort if that's what it is of steering things in a better direction eventually once it becomes habitual ceases to be uncomfortable at all, and instead it starts to feel like a healthy amount of control.

TIP

'Think forwards' to beat inertia today and reap the reward of avoiding the bigger catastrophe tomorrow, plus as a bonus once that is embedded in your approach, a healthier culture of seeing a hand on the steering wheel as a robust and flourishing way of running your business, in preference to the imagined comfort of doing nothing being better.

****

26

Customer care and dealing with complaints

When you look at how to contact a company, only to find no e-mail address or phone number on the website, or possibly worse ten e-mails or numbers (without it being easily obvious which is the appropriate one to use), and you find that the order confirmation e-mail is from a 'no reply' account, what thoughts does your mind drift off to? In an instant, your perception of a business can go south. It is bad enough that they've delivered the wrong thing, or not delivered, or not showed up on time or done the right thing (or whatever the issue is), but doubly bad that even reaching out to them to explore the issue now looks impossible by design. Make it easy for customers to contact you and fast to get to the solution.

Your e-mail bounces back from the 'no reply' inbox, because you had hit reply to the e-mail they sent to you, only to find they don't want your reply, so you spend ten minutes searching for the right number, call it, and the recorded message declares, *"our offices are now closed. We operate between 9 and 5 daily. Thank you for calling."* Why didn't the e-mail and website mention the times when calls are answered? Why didn't it give an e-mail or web chat for outside those hours? Why not operate a helpline over longer hours, especially when you can envisage customers needing you at certain times. A 9-5 helpline, for example, is probably no use to customers who need a day job to pay for what you are selling to them.

You call back the next day, after 9am, to be greeted with another recording: *"if you wish to place a new order, press 1; if you wish to enquire about an outstanding order, press 2; for public relations, press 3; for complaints, press 4; for anything else, press 5."* You want to speak about the wrong item having been delivered: which of the offered options is the appropriate one?! Foresee client needs and make it easy for them to get to the right person to sort it out.

When you finally do get the 'right' person at the end of the phone, they say the system doesn't show your order as delivered yet and before they can go into the order to help it needs to show as delivered; they suggest you call back another time!

You decide to e-mail instead. The auto acknowledgement reply doesn't tell you in what timescale to expect a response. One hasn't been forthcoming 5 days later.

You bin the goods and decide never to use the company again.

You tell at least ten of your friends in the weeks that follow. They trust your judgement, are horrified by the experience, and they swerve the business too.

You might, if you could be bothered, sue. Which would, in Court fees, costs and interest, cost the company more.

Does a business ever win by having poor customer support? No. Financially not because customers do not return. Reputationally not because your reviews and word of mouth will be awful. And not even from a point of internal cost cutting either; a process in which customers get lost or can't easily reach you and which takes longer probably costs you more because they'll end up in the wrong place with the need to be re-directed, or there will be multiple touch points when a good process would involve just one. Make it easy for people to contact you. And fast for them to get the outcome they want.

If you think in business you are winning because you've invented a process which has cut down on the number of contacts from customers and thereby saved your staff time, have a second think about that. You think you are winning because customers who want to contact you cannot do so. If that's a win, imagine what a loss might look like.

And treat customers as you would want to be treated when dealing with the reason for them getting in touch. Have people that can understand the issue immediately. And resolve it soon after. Understanding and solutions will enhance a customer's view of your business; a lack of those things will keep customers away.

A debt collection company once reviewed some debts for a customer. It closed debts and took the view that there were many without prospects of success but in respect of which there was in fact good prospects of success. The supplier had failed to recover money which the client thought they should have, and thus the client felt let down. There had been some mistakes.

The supplier's instinct was to interrupt the client's complaint, as if it was something to be quickly buried rather than aired: *"we can sit here all day going through the detail, and we might not agree; shall we just jump straight to what you want and I can tell you if we are on the same page..."* The interruption with a view to stifling the complaint rather than hearing it was wrong. It is best to allow a complaining customer to vent fully. Don't jump in too soon. They need to get it off their chest. And you will need to hear it all in order to understand properly and come up with a proper response. Not just for the sake of the particular complaint, but also to see if you can learn something which might enable you to make your business better.

The supplier's first response when the client's complaint was aired was, among other things, *"look at the thickness of the files; it isn't as if we haven't tried."* And it seemingly meant those words sincerely: it thought that a pile of correspondence was a good result even if it had achieved absolutely nothing. In the client's eyes, this actually made the situation even worse than an already bad one, because not only had the case handlers not really made an effort, which was the suspicion for having not succeeded in the claims, but even worse than that they had made an effort and still failed where they should have succeeded. A bad excuse is worse than no excuse at all. Would you return to an incapable supplier? Would you recommend them to anyone else who might ask you for a recommendation in future?

The supplier said that while no fault was accepted, it would send a (modest) sum of money to try to conclude the matter, and the client could take or leave it. This left the client feeling excluded from the decision-making process. And disappointed at still feeling left short compared to the outcome it should have had if the claims management company had handled the claims competently in the first place.

No changes were made back at the claims management firm. If there are lessons to be learned, make the changes necessary, if any, to prevent a reoccurrence.

The lessons for the firm were:

1. A better synergy were needed between client and supplier. The firm thought 'light touch' was the right approach; the client was expecting a good job.
2. Staff needed training to give them a better toolkit to tackle claims, and do a better job than the client could have done itself
3. Supervision could be tighter, to prevent quality lapses
4. IT could be slicker, to help busy teams manage claims

None of these things were done. The potential lessons were not even considered. The business could have learned these lessons, improved itself, and reaped the rewards in terms of more satisfied customers in future and the additional work an improved reputation might generate.

The business could have seen it as a small price to pay for all that useful feedback, enabling such improvements, to offer the client £30k instead of the £20k in dispute. It could have apologised to the client, stated the lessons learned and positive changes made as a result, thanked the client, paid over and above what the client was asking for, and scheduled future meetings to ensure the client remained delighted with the new service. A customer wants a supplier it can trust. An opportunity to show you will (more than) do the right thing if anything does ever go wrong is not one to waste: use it to plant in the customer's mind the idea that it can trust you to demonstrate integrity when there is a blip.

The claims management company did not retain the complaining client. Its reputation remained rather average in the market. It eventually failed and went into liquidation. It thought complaints were a drag and were to be rejected to keep the money in the company's account rather than 'losing' money to complaining clients. It thought that improvements would be only a drag on profitability. That approach in the long term compromised its very survival. Perhaps counterintuitively to that business, it would have profited by giving the customer more than it wanted, and by making the improvements the complaint highlighted as desirable. Turning the pain of a complaint into an opportunity to delight a client and simultaneously to make changes to improve the business is the best approach to feedback.

Some complaints have caused me as a customer never to return to a business. When a business refuses to admit the mistake it has made, is reluctant to do anything at all about it, and only acts through gritted teeth and with a scoff, it is unlikely to attract many good returning customers. However, when a business uses a complaint as an opportunity to delight then it can enhance the customer experience and as a result win life-long customers, and promoters. Imagine buying a very expensive vase for a wedding gift for a very good friend, only to find it chipped on one side, and a large air bubble in the glass on the other side. If the seller said the defects are small and they wouldn't usually do anything, and if you want a refund or exchange you'll have to pay the £25 return courier fee, how would you feel? You would probably feel negative about that business. You would only buy again cautiously or reluctantly. You can't trust that they'll say or do the right thing. On the other hand, what if the seller said we've refunded you, keep the item for free, and here's 20% off your next purchase, you might feel more positive about that business than you did in the first place. Something went wrong, but we accept that in life sometimes things do go wrong. But this business used it as an opportunity to show you they will say and do the right thing. It is a business you can trust. Now the first business owner might laugh at the second business owner and say that business is throwing money away and won't be around for very long. But if the second business wins most customers in the market, and goes on to secure regular repeat business, who wins financially? Doing the right thing when things go wrong is not just morally satisfactory, it in the long run causes the better financial performance too.

TIP

Customer service is important. Even a business that manufactures or sells superb goods can be brought down by poor customer service. If you went to a friend's house and they wouldn't answer the door until you'd chosen a reason for visiting from 9 options, if they then made you queue for half an hour, and if they then said come back tomorrow, would you visit again? No. The same is true in business.

Complaints or negative feedback are one of the biggest opportunities to find a way of bettering your business by improving in response to the feedback. And at the same time an opportunity to make a customer a bigger fan than they were before things went wrong. Don't waste that potential. Learn from the feedback and make the business better. Wow the customer by dealing with the feedback well, and they will love you more than if things had never gone wrong in the first place.

****

Afterword

There is no single answer to the question what makes a business succeed. Successful businesses get many things right, including those things touched on in this book and many more besides. But what sets the best businesses apart is a refusal to stop at just 'good enough.' Instead the best businesses ask every day how can be improved. They ask, 'what can be better?' They certainly don't complacently wait for a complaint to be made to spur them into action. Each of the chapters in this book is just one instance of how a business might be better by following the lessons of each example rather than ignoring them. If it sounds like hard work, it can actually become quite a rewarding way to approach things. If something feels boring or stale or doesn't feel great, well find out why, and make it better!

Whether you are launching a business, already managing one, or just looking to be better and more entrepreneurial in your work life, keep learning, and I hope it's an ongoing journey full of luck, learning, and realising your full potential. Whatever your place in business, in whatever sector, and whatever role, never settle for just good enough. Keep asking how can it be better...!

9 781680 533279